AN OWL ON EVERY POST

AN OWL
ON EVERY
POST

by Sanora Babb

The McCall Publishing Company

NEW YORK

To my husband
JAMES WONG HOWE
and my sister
DOROTHY

Published simultaneously in Canada by
Doubleday Canada Ltd., Toronto.

Library of Congress Catalog Card Number: 75-122113

SBN 8415-0037-1

The McCall Publishing Company
230 Park Avenue, New York, N.Y. 10017

Printed in the United States of America

Design by Tere LoPrete

". . . a land that seemed to be grieving over something —a kind of sadness, loneliness in a deathly quiet . . ."

BOB BEVERLY in *Hobo of the Rangeland*

AN OWL ON EVERY POST

I

ALL THE WAY on the train from the Indian country of Oklahoma
to the flat plains of Colorado east of the Rocky Mountains, my
mother and I were sad; she to leave household and friends, and a
town, however small; I, to leave my pinto pony and the Oto
Indians near Red Rock, my other family, my other home. It was
early autumn, 1913. My sister was happy: Her whole world was
Papa and he was waiting for us at the end of the railroad in
Lamar. Somewhere back of us in the slow mixed train of a handful of passengers and cars of coal, flour, lard, canned food supplies, and other necessities for this isolated place, was a freight
car in which our piano was coming with us. As he would in our
many moves to come, my father had commanded that nothing be
brought along. In one of her rare self-assertions, my mother had
refused to leave her new piano. She played and sang rather
well.

Having grown up in a large comfortable home in a lovely town
of tree-shaded brick walks, flower-fragrant summers, woods and

meadows and a stream for playground; having since her marriage
lived in somewhat less comfort and much uncertainty, though
never in a place without trees, she was utterly unprepared for
the desolation viewed from the train window. Even the com-
panionship of her piano could not keep back the tears.

The lackluster autumn landscape was like an old gray carpet
spread to the far, far circling horizon. There was nothing more to
see. This was an empty land. A primordial loneliness was on it;
the train carried us backward in time.

Our Grandfather Alonzo lived here, somewhere in that gray
waste. He was "proving up" a government claim, 160 acres, a
quarter of a section, all to be his for improving it, which meant
building a dwelling, paying taxes, and living on it five years.
After its hard-won possession he lost it to taxes ten years later,
unable to raise crops without water. The government had opened
these margin lands for settlement, and so powerfully inviting is
the ownership of land that people came; many left, a few
remained. Grandfather Alonzo, a silent, inward man, impractical
and visionary, so taken with the future that he had failed to write
of the present in his letters to Papa, had convinced him that he
should sell his bakery and invest in 320 acres of grazing land for
sale. Finally, Papa had bought the land sight unseen through
his father, spending all his cash, banking on the next summer's
crops to launch us into agricultural prosperity while enjoying the
wonders of pioneering again. We were to live with Grandfather
Alonzo until we could build a sod house after the first crops
were in. While other parts of the United States moved swiftly
ahead, the hopeful or desperate people who filed claims on these
high western grazing lands were plunged a hundred years backward in our history, to live and struggle again like the early settlers in other states.

As we watched from the train windows, we did not know this,
but I am sure my mother felt that her young life had come to a
dismal end. She was twenty-four, my father thirty-two; I was
seven and my sister four. We were well-dressed and rounded with
good food and health. Whatever deprivations we had known,
they were not material.

The bell rang, the train slowed, and we looked out into great
pens of whiteface cattle driven in from the range, waiting to be

loaded for market. The pens seemed endless. The prescient bawling of the cattle added a strange dimension to the already strange
atmosphere. The little station slid alongside and we saw Papa,
whom we had not seen for five long months, watching for a sight
of us. My sister ran ahead and leaped into his arms. We four had
a happy reunion until my mother mentioned the piano.

"We're fifty miles from here. I'll have to hire a wagon to come
after it! Goddamn."

"Oh, Walt! I couldn't leave my piano."

We did not see the town of Lamar, but were bustled at once
into a black Ford touring car with all curtains fastened against the
cold wind. Luggage was tied to the steps and the back. One other
passenger sat with the driver, another in the back seat with us.
As I was the last getting in, there was no room for me. My
father was holding my sister on his lap, and he commanded me to
sit on the floor among the feet. I was angry and humiliated. I
wanted to see the land we passed, but dark was already rushing
by as if the night wind had turned black. The single dirt road
I had seen ran straight on level plain; we met no one. Cold air
came up through the cracks of the floor boards, but the silent
company above gave off body heat.

In spite of discomfort and my lowly position among the high-
buttoned shoes, my sense of adventure began to reassert itself;
I was traveling again and I could hardly wait for tomorrow in a
new place. But a new place suggested an old one, and I began to
think of my pony, who must be missing me on his bare back, my
moccasined feet holding softly against his "painted" flanks. I
would never again ride him fast over the Indian lands or to and
from the town of Red Rock; I would never again be known or
called by my Indian name: Little Cheyenne Riding Like the
Wind. I tried to imagine that I was back there with them, in old
Edie's big lap or held tenderly against Chief Black Hawk's to-
bacco-smelly chest, hearing his heart thunder in my ear over his
long silences, or his rare monosyllables of love. I cried myself
to sleep thinking of the friends I had lived with and played
with for three years, especially of Shy Quail and Young Man
Afraid of His Horse. He was afraid only when set upon his first
horse. At the powwows, the three of us had raced bareback on our
horses, an eagle feather in our headbands, wanting to be like the

braves. I had seen not one woman or man at the station of Lamar with long black braided hair, wearing bright blankets. Not one. This was a strange place.

My mother shook me gently awake and we got out of the car, weary and stiff from the long ride. Our traveling companions went their way. The tiny village of Two Buttes was dark with sleep. A lighted window of the small place where we stopped beckoned us to spend the night. Mama suggested it.

"There's no hotel here," Papa said. "We have to go on." He had arranged it with the driver. "We'll just stretch our muscles."

We could hardly bear the thought of still another journey; we had only napped on the train since leaving Oklahoma. But Papa's word was law.

A woman in nightclothes opened the lighted door and looked at us one by one.

"Want a cup of java?"

"Oh, yes, oh, thanks, thanks!" Mama said.

"Come in out of the cold wind, all of you," the woman said, and we went in, the driver rubbing his hands and doing a grim little dance to get his kinks out.

"I'll fix the girls some warm milk."

She handed Mama a lighted lantern and showed us the long path on the hard ground that led to an outhouse with a crescent and star carved in its door. When we came back, the warm drinks were ready, the simple kitchen fragrant with coffee. A loganberry pie was cut.

"Couldn't heat the pie," the woman said. "It'd take a year to heat the oven. Fire's been out for hours. I just heated up the coffee and milk with cedar bark."

That accounted for the other good fragrance in the room. The warm drinks, the good pie, the woman's stern kindness were all like a banquet.

Over her honest protests, Papa paid her, and on the way out she dropped the silver dollar warmed by her hand into my back collar. It slid all the way down into the leg of my long underwear. Because her act was so private, I gave the dollar to my mother in secret, and she would have passed it back to Papa if I had not given her a warning nudge.

Outside again, Mama asked, "Who is that nice woman?"

"I don't know," Papa said.

"I reckon she heard us getting ready to take another jaunt," the driver said. "Now and then she does that."

We drove away into the pitch-black night seven more miles. I sat with the driver, awake and eager to see. Now and then I was rewarded by the sudden flash of eyes like two round piercing fires in the dark.

"Wolves," the driver told me. "They ain't afraid. Coyotes circle around." He called them *ki-oats*.

Often the smell of skunks came into the car, and once I saw one bounding off the road, its beautiful black and white brush like a plume.

"Come tomorrow, you want to look at the prairie dog towns," he said. "But watch out for the rattlesnakes. This country is full of rattlesnakes. But they coil and rattle and give fair warning before they strike."

I heard my mother gasp.

"Tarantulas and centipedes, too. Look out for them. Lots of wild things out here. This land's belonged to them so long, they think they own it. Out on the range, look out for bulls. Some of 'em real mean. No fences here yet. Well, just a few, but the Russian thistles pile up on 'em and the cattle walk right over the fences. Some wildcats and such down along Horse Creek in the canyons."

I was beginning to like the sound of this place, when I heard my mother say with relief, "A creek!"

"That's where we get our water," Papa said. "It's two miles south of us."

"Isn't there a well?"

"There isn't anything," Papa said grimly.

After that we rode in silence through the blackness, too weary to exclaim at the stars straight ahead where the sky curved down to the horizon.

"What is that light on the ground up ahead?" Mama asked.

"That's it."

As we turned into the gate, the headlights flashed on the low peak of shingles and a small window flush to the ground. A black shepherd dog was barking. A long slab of light suddenly rose from some depth; a cellar door fell back, and a tall thin man came up the steps and into the yard. He stood apart for a moment, then came forward and greeted us with no words at all. He did not seem unfriendly but he only nodded. I looked at his long dark face and black eyes and black hair. A full black mustache drooped over his upper lip and mouth. I liked him at once, his darkness and his silence. He was like an Indian.

Mama pushed my sister and me toward him and said, "Say hello to your Grandfather Alonzo." Then, to him, she said, "They are terribly tired, Alonzo."

The driver left and we stood in the dark yard for a moment without speaking. The wind had died, and the silence was immense. It filled the world and fell upon us like an omen. We moved toward the slab of light. The dog wagged about us.

"Go to sleep, Bounce. You can get acquainted in the morning."

We hesitated at the steep cement steps as if we could not believe what we saw. Finally, my father started down in guilty impatience. We followed. We stepped onto a hard earthen floor and saw at once that the walls were of earth. The room was very small, its only furniture a bed and a wire cot, a small wooden table with boxes for chairs, a tiny, two-hole monkey stove, and beside it a box filled with dried cow chips. Standing on a box, we could look out the window onto the ground and feel a part of the miniature life of ants and beetles and anything that crawled. The possibilities of this unusual land were growing.

My mother was biting her lips to keep from bursting into tears. No letters had described this dugout or its isolation.

"Where will we sleep?" she asked.

"The three of us in the big bed, and Cheyenne will have to sleep with Dad on the cot."

"How!"

"Well, he doesn't like being crowded either."

"This is the limit," Mama said bravely.

"It's the best we can do. Dad talked me into buying a gold-brick. I can't even sell it. Thousands of acres of free range all around, and government claims. I'm broke. I was a damn fool to listen to him."

Grandfather Alonzo came down the steps on that remark. "That's all I've heard since you came," he said quietly. "Remember, you didn't want to be tied down to the claim years. It's late. We should all go to sleep." He turned the wick low in the oil lamp, and we undressed in the shadows that darted tall over the walls as we moved. Although the air above ground was sharp and dry, in the dugout a dank earth dampness pressed into our breath, chilled our bones. The slant door had been let down. We were trapped.

"This place is like a grave," Papa said.

Grandfather turned back the covers of his narrow cot, all rough blankets, no sheets. He got into bed and turned his face toward the wall. I lay down gingerly, disliking all of our indoor life before it had begun, eager for morning, to escape into the clean air.

"Bakery gone and all my money in some worthless land with a future!" Papa said. "Future a hundred years off. So what can we do but live here and try to raise a crop of broomcorn?"

"We can go to sleep. I'm so tired I don't care where I am just now. We'll talk tomorrow."

"Are you glad to see me?" Papa asked her.

"Yes, I am," and she meant it.

In the deep wild silence, I heard the coyotes yapping. Then a night owl: hoooooo-hoo. I listened to those good sounds. Then I heard the fast soft ticks of little feet running up and down the walls. Once a thump on my blanket and the feet continuing on the floor. I wanted to wake up Papa to protect us, but I knew that I must keep still and perhaps I would sleep, perhaps morning would come.

Then something bit me. Without thinking, I scratched the bite, felt a small fat bug, and smelled a revolting odor. I cried out; I could not help it. Mama was instantly awake, out of her bed.

"Light the lamp," Grandfather advised, "and they'll go away for a time."

Papa leaped cursing from the bed and lighted the oil lamp. Even in its dim glow we saw the oval brown bugs running over our pillows and up the walls, hurrying away from the light.

"What are they?" my mother asked in a sickened voice.

"Bedbugs. They came in the new lumber. Dad's lived alone so long he doesn't care, didn't even try to get rid of them."

"You did?" Grandfather said to the wall.

"Well, I will," Mama said with terrible determination. "As soon as it's daylight." She reached for my hand. "We'll sleep in the wagon."

"It's too cold," Papa said.

"Bring Marcy and the covers." She had never spoken in this way before; it was against her nature. Papa, amazed, obeyed her.

"I wouldn't," Grandfather suggested. "The wolves—"

"Bother the wolves," she said, and went up the steps so blindly that she bumped her head. Papa pushed up the door, and it seemed that the stars were falling down upon us.

2

We were up at dawn, a cool, frosty dawn. We saw the gray fields of night on the plain, tall like the once-tall grass. We watched the big sky turn pink and orange, then blue. The air was of such purity that we stood breathing deeply for the simple pleasure of breathing. Its fragrance was unlike the softer, leafy air we had known. Strong plants that lived in a land of little rain gave into the winds their pungent smells, sagebrush more powerful than all others. We turned around and around to see the full circle of horizon, the perfect meeting of earth and sky. Two pointed buttes to the northwest were the only blemish on the plain. Their hulks had been thrown up from the earth in digging a silver mine. We were at once in a grand and endless space, and enclosed, locked in.

My mother began her new life with remarkable courage. She was a girl, really, in her mid-twenties, small, fine-boned, and pretty, with physical strength and energy concealed in her gentle ways. That first morning after breakfast she asked the men to bring everything from the dugout into the sun. Almost the only preparation Papa had made for her was to stretch a clothesline between two cedar posts. On this she hung all the bedding and clothes. The mattresses were placed on the bare yard. The iron bedstead and springs and the wire cot she cleaned with coal oil, and she set their feet in little food cans of the oil. Everything was doused and scrubbed and aired; the two small windows were open all day. We all slept out that night.

In the morning Mama made a paste of flour and water and papered the earthen walls with *Denver Posts*. The floor was earth, but it was as hard as stone and swept clean.

The days were, for autumn, still pleasantly warm. We took our food and all the bedding and our empty water barrels, two for the horses and one for us, and drove to the creek. There Mama and Papa washed the quilts and blankets and spread them on the huge rocks to dry. We unhitched the horses, Fred and Dip, and turned them loose to enjoy the running water and the presence of cottonwood trees. As the approach to the creek went down below a precipice, its trees could not be seen from our farm. They and the stream were like a gift to us all. When the work was done, we bathed and Papa swam in wild high spirits, shouting with unrestrained pleasure, inviting us to a water fight against him. No matter how the three of us flung ourselves upon him, tugged at him, climbed upon him, we could not down him in the water, and were all ducked, laughing and struggling against his strength. The horses raised their heads and looked on as if we were creatures strange to them. After that the bathing trip to the creek was a weekly adventure except in winter. Drinking water was hauled more frequently. During blizzards, Papa chopped the ice to bail from the water below. If it froze solid, we melted the ice at home on the little monkey stove, but more often, if the snow had not been blown from the ground, we melted that. Now while the days were crisp and the sun kinder than in summer, we had to prepare, for winter lasted long, and we were soon to learn how ferocious its storms, how bitter its cold, how inhumanely isolated our lives.

Though the five of us were stuffed into the tiny room below

ground, the room was now clean. Because we had not one corner of privacy, we children spent much time out of doors, exploring the patch of chopped cane to the south of the dugout, the open fields to the north and east, the hard bare yard where the broom-corn harvesters had baled the crop and left a dry lake of seeds and straws. We ventured into the barn, a small building roofed with cane, where Grandfather Alonzo retreated by day, aloof, humiliated, criticized by the swift changes; he mended harness, cared for the horses, and read a book. Papa had warned us not to go near him (and yet he and I shared a cot!) because of the vivid red spots on his face.

Papa was busy, perhaps repairing fence; but it was Mama whose hard work seldom gave her a chance to emerge into the good air. Now and then she engaged in her favorite pleasure: writing letters to relatives and friends, a pleasure that our poverty soon made a rare and infrequent event. We had no cash for two-cent stamps. In those first days, while she was making the room more livable, she was also rearranging every piece of furniture to make a place for her piano. At last she cleared a space; the piano would fill the east wall to the right of the door, its stool to serve also at the small handmade table with its oilcloth cover and tin dishes. As our household goods had been sold or given away, we were forced to adapt ourselves from china to tin, as we were forced to disremember various other fastidious habits.

The second Saturday arrived in what seemed years after our arrival; we were going to town! Not the town of the train's end, but the one of our brief stopover in the dead of night. Any town would have been welcome, so hungry were we all for the sight of other human beings. Grandfather Alonzo must be excepted; he went to town only when absolute necessity forced him.

The previous day we drove to the creek and bathed, a delightful expedition marred by Papa's harsh words to Grandfather.

"If we're going to have to live together, you've got to keep clean."

Grandfather clucked his tongue, his habitual attempt at peace.

"Get in the wagon! You're getting old and dirty."

"Not so old," Grandfather said. "Not yet sixty."

"All the worse."

Grandfather removed the endgate of the wagon bed and mo-

tioned for my sister and me to sit with him there, our backs
to the high seat in front. Beside Papa, Mama sat holding a bundle of clean clothes for all.

"Tomorrow in town," Papa called back, "you're going to the
doctor. I don't know what you've got on your face."

At this Grandfather looked sidewise at me, giving a little nod
that expected my understanding. The sympathy I had hidden
burst like a bud in my heart.

"I sometimes walk to the creek alone," he said to me in a low
voice. "He can think what he likes."

It was not in my nature to enter a confederacy, and I sensed
that he did not wish that of me; but it was true we each needed
a friend. While my father boasted that I had a "wild spirit" like
his own, he most obviously favored Marcy.

Mama favored us all with her care and concern, swallowed her
frustrations in favor of an atmosphere of kindness, and when she
failed, kept stubbornly quiet until she could find a free moment
and a private place to cry. In summer, when the cane was tall
near the dugout, I sometimes surprised her there sobbing. To my
questions she replied, "Oh, nothing." Once she cried out, "I'm
bitterly lonesome!" giving me my first sure insight into the difference of our two worlds. I had not forgotten my Indian friends
or my pinto pony, but I had begun to like this land and its ways.
I felt close to its animals and birds and sparse growing things, its
silence, even its loneliness. Its loneliness stretched my soul beyond
my years to a mysterious sense of a time when I should reach that
far land's end and lift up the sky to enter the lives and the worlds
I had no need to know until then.

On the next day after our baths at the creek, we rose at our
usual dawn hour and dressed in our finest town clothes. We
looked out of place in the dugout, unsuited to the old wagon,
and our high holiday spirits rippled over the past dissensions as
the crystal water of Horse Creek sparkled over its pebbled bed.

Papa looked at Mama with admiration and said, "You belong
in a carriage."

"By Jove, it's so," Grandfather Alonzo said. "Pretty as a prairie
flower."

Even Bounce, the dog, was excited. He trotted along behind
when he wasn't chasing rabbits.

We sat on quilts spread over a cushion of fodder. Grandfather, having become a third party, had made himself a short-legged spring chair on which he sat in the back with us, now and then calling up advice to Papa on the dispositions of the horses.

"Dip is the plodder, Fred is the hard fast worker. Rein him back a little before he tires Dip. It isn't that Dip is hanging back. That's his way."

Papa turned his head and smiled at Mama; it was plain that Grandfather had said this before, perhaps many times. But he loved his horses; they had been his only friends in the years alone. He spoke to them in the barn about their foibles and assured them he understood, as he had foibles of his own. He fed them better than he fed himself, curried them, and visited them when they were not on the range cropping grass. They were so trustworthy and fond of him that he set them free there without hobbles, and when they were ready to return, Fred lifed the wire loop from the gateposts and let themselves back in. Grandfather had to watch out for that trick when he had a stand of young broomcorn or maize lest stock grazing on the range overrun his fields.

Less than a hundred people lived in the town of Two Buttes, a village really, if the term were used in the West, which it is not. We unhitched our horses in an open feed lot near the general store, tied them to the wagon, put down their feed and water, and left them, to go about our day.

Sure that Grandfather would not see the doctor if left to his own actions, we went there first and listened to every word. Dr. Burtis took one look at Grandfather and declared that he had scurvy, explained that his diet was lacking, and demanded to know what he ate.

"Mostly a flour and water pancake fried with a bit of lard, and once in a while some beans." Grandfather called his pancake hardtack; it was as big as a plate and an inch thick, fried one day and broken off and eaten as many days as it lasted. It became rather like a huge thick cracker. We were eating it every day, but Mama had been adding whatever else she could from the small larder of cans.

The doctor nodded. This was the familiar food of the poor homesteader, especially the lone man. He asked about a spring garden.

"No well yet."

"If nature has provided any wild plants here for a man to eat, it must be her secret," Dr. Burtis said. "But we should be finding out about such things, as many of you people are going to starve to death on this hardtack. Lemons are a luxury, but they are a well-known cure from sailing-ship times."

Grandfather nodded without comment.

Dr. Burtis gazed at my mother with the pleasure of seeing a well-dressed pretty woman in such a place, and addressed himself to her. "Prepare anything green you find growing that isn't poisonous. I'm not yet familiar with the plants of this godforsaken place, and without the Indians we'll have a hard time finding out. Eat your potatoes with their overcoats on. Careful on the salt pork too." He spoke to Grandfather again. "Lucky your gums are not yet in bad shape."

Grandfather drew his leather snap purse from his pocket and was ready to pay.

"The cure is all up to you," Dr. Burtis said. "Try to drill a well, and bring me some fresh vegetables next spring."

The doctor stood there in his book-cluttered office, with a back door open a crack revealing an even more book-cluttered living quarter, the place of a man alone. According to a local tale, the doctor had his own very personal reasons for living on the plains.

Outside, perhaps to make up for his cruelty, Papa said, "Now that Ginny is here, she'll fix you better food."

"With what?" Grandfather asked.

"We still have a little money, Dad, damn little; but it's a cinch we can't drill a well."

"Why not?" Marcy wanted to know.

"Costs too much. Have to go too deep to hit water here. No well, no garden. Hell of a place."

"Let's go to the post office, Walt; I can hardly wait."

At the general delivery window Mama was handed mail from relatives and friends. Her delight was so intense that she shuffled through the letters again and again, laughing and turning in a slow dreamy whirl.

"I won't open them now. I'll save them for that lonesome old place."

She let me buy stamps and drop her own letters into the slot. That little post office had magic in its barred windows suggesting treasure and in the mail that could only be given, never bought.

That day, after Mama's first mail, we walked once up and down the one short street of Two Buttes. Men in clean farm clothes or cowboy outfits, women in long fresh gingham dresses and ruffled sunbonnets passed us and all stared discreetly at our stranger-faces and town clothes.

Mama said, "We won't dress this way again. They'll think we're putting on airs."

A few persons stopped us and inquired, "Are you Alonzo's new kin?"

Alonzo had gone about his own business after seeing the doctor, so that out of his presence one man said, "Keeps to himself. Hope you folks will come visit us. Anytime. Latch key's out. Woman will *sure* be glad to see you."

We went back to the wagon to eat the lunch we had brought and there met Grandfather leading Fred and Dip away to the blacksmith's, where they were to get new shoes. He had been saving money for a long time and we could see that he was in good spirits to have accomplished this for his horses. When Mama offered him our usual dull fare, he said he had been to the café. At this announcement, Marcy begged of Papa that we go there too. Mama held the food, ready to put it back in its basket at once, her large blue eyes lighting at the prospect of a change. Papa's whole face radiated the pleasure he was about to bestow upon us.

"Come on," he said gaily, "put that hardtack away. We've still got a little money."

He led us to the Royal Café, a small narrow place with a lunch counter and stools, upon which we perched with delight. Restaurant dinners of the recent past faded from memory in our eagerness for the festivity of "eating out" in this dingy smoke-stained café. Papa gave us a look, the one he gave us in public, which meant "mind your manners." An enormous woman came from the open door to the kitchen, wiped the clean counter, and stood before us, drawing conclusions, her direct eyes friendly, the dark hairs on her perspiring upper lip adding to the handsomeness of her face.

"So this is your family? Pretty as a picture." She smiled at Mama. "How come you let your man homestead?"

Before Mama could answer this jesting impertinence, Papa asked, "Seen any ghosts lately, Mrs. Denny?"

"That I have, and don't you be making light of him, the poor devil."

"I'm not; I saw my mother's ghost when I was a boy, and ask

my wife here if I didn't see her sister before we knew she had died, died in a town five hundred miles away."

Mama nodded yes without conviction, because she had never seen a ghost and hoped that she never would.

"Who is the 'poor devil'?" I asked politely.

"Well, that's a dear child, and it serves me right," the woman said, laughing. "The 'poor devil' is my husband. He was an old nester, older than me, and he passed over, and now and then, dear, he comes back to see how I'm getting along. It's nothing to be afraid of. It sort of comforts me." She was speaking to Mama and Papa but she was gazing at me in a sweet way.

"What is an old nester, please?" I asked.

"An old nester is an old homesteader who has been here a long time before these new ones. When he died, I come to town and opened this little place. I couldn't abide that farm alone."

"I should think not," Mama said.

"My goodness, I expect you folks want something to eat and here I am visiting with you."

"We enjoy it," Mama and Papa said at once.

"Your dad was just in and ate a big dinner. Said about two words. I'll fix you something as nice as I can with what I've got." She went to the kitchen without asking for an order and very shortly came out with plates of thin fried steak, fried potatoes and onions, their white discs lightly browned, and tomatoes stewed with butter, and pieces of bread. She poured steaming coffee for Mama and Papa and set before my sister and me glasses of milk.

"Hope you like my country cooking," she said, looking at Mama's velvet hat, and withdrew to the kitchen, singing and clattering about until she reappeared with a heated apple pie. "Now you people enjoy yourselves. I've got to grind some beef. Men'll be in here wanting fresh hamburgers."

"I'll pay you now, then," Papa said.

"It says how much on the mirror," she said. "Just leave it on the counter." She turned back a moment. "I'm proud to meet your family. Come and see me."

When we entered the general store to buy our week's supplies, the owner, whom we came to know as humorous but moody Mr. Tullery, stared at my mother, as did everyone present, in a discreet way. She was uncomfortable but Papa was proud of his family. With us he was proud, critical, teasing. He would shout and storm, or ignore us completely, to withdraw into a sad, thoughtful, sometimes ominous mood. But there were no ordinary quiet times with him. He was a magnetic man, arousing others to his own emotions. Where he went, others seemed to light up as if his presence sent a new charge into their faithful humdrum batteries.

In the center of the high-ceilinged store was a large potbellied heater and in a rough circle around it a number of chairs and stools. Farmers sat together speaking of the dry climate, of dryland farming, the crops, the difficulty of making a living. Sometimes they laughed in quiet ways. Perhaps the great hush of the unpeopled land made them soft-spoken. Papa sat down among them and began speaking of far-off events of a far-off world. As their thoughts left their hard lives, their voices became more lively, their laughter more frequent.

Farm women were buying from their lists, charging their purchases until next harvest. A few of them were at the dry-goods counter lingering over materials for coats and dresses. My sister and I followed Mama to the grocery side, and Mr. Tullery put up her sparse order with unconcealed delight and polite questions and comments. Suddenly, as if a moment of reckless daring had overwhelmed her, she bought cans of vegetables and fruits with the secret dollar I had relayed to her our first night there. We had not yet asked for credit, or Papa had not, and Mr. Tullery received our money with as much surprise as gratification. He reached into a large glass jar of candy and handed Marcy and me each a striped stick, for which we thanked him; then, hesitating a moment, he handed another to Mama. He nodded his head in such a way as to make the gesture seem like a bow and said, "With all due respect, you are also just a little girl."

Mama blushed and smiled, and bit the end off the stick of candy. Marcy hid hers in a pocket for another day. I knew she would eat only a little at a time, finishing the stick just before the next Saturday in town. I bit off a piece of my candy and inadvertently made a crunch that was heard in an instant of stillness. Papa looked at me and stood up.

"We have to go," he excused himself, and called over to Mr. Tullery, "I'll be back later to pick up the order."

Outside he scolded Mama and me. "Eating in public!"

"Oh, fiddlesticks!" Mama said without impatience. We put our candy in our clean handkerchiefs and into our pockets.

"We're going visiting," Papa announced. "We'll go see the Shibleys, friends I've made. They have an invalid son who's about dead. Some company will do them good."

Both Marcy and I were afraid of sick persons, the ones who were in bed, remote strangers submerged in a life unknown to us.

We hung back, watching a large anthill, the great red ants hurrying, carrying prey, sticks, enormous loads they put down and picked up again, moving in an ordered, inexorable way toward their destination.

Papa turned. "Come on!"

We went.

3

WHEN MR. SHIBLEY opened the door and shouted, "Walt, you rascal!" Mrs. Shibley came running up behind her husband and said, "Open the screen, Grif!"

"Walt knows how to open this screen any old day." He flung it open and the fringed paper tacked on against the summer flies rippled like lace in the autumn wind. Mrs. Shibley held out her arms urging us.

She looked directly into Mama's eyes and said in a tender voice, "You're Ginny."

"Yes," Mama said as if she had been told her name at last.

Mrs. Shibley told us our names, my sister's and mine, suiting her tone to her quick impression of our ways. To Marcy, painfully shy away from home, she sang a private welcome. Marcy leaned against Papa's legs for safety and, looking down, tried bravely to utter a polite word of response. No word came. Mrs. Shibley behaved as if she had been greeted and touched Marcy's blond hair. Then a flaw appeared in this perfection, a flaw that I could not immediately forgive.

"Walt, you cannot let this child go around with the ridiculous name of Cheyenne."

"She has a real name," my mother said and was about to speak it.

"Walt didn't tell me," Mrs. Shibley interrupted. "What is it?"

"Cheyenne," Papa said firmly.

Mrs. Shibley's face went blank for a moment and then she laughed. "Just like you, Walter."

Mama smiled at us all. We already had that sense of being in league with one another no matter what differences occurred at home. So as not to hurt Mrs. Shibley's feelings or my own, Mama would tell her my name in private.

Mr. Shibley was standing aside observing. He winked at me, a large consoling wink, and said, "Heap big squaw." This confused me; I liked his friendliness but not his words. I was dead serious about my Indian family and he was not.

He saved us all by wheeling fast and recklessly in from another room, his wheelchair coming to an expert stop in our midst. Appearing both shy, sensitive perhaps, and at ease, his weak voice crowed with delight and welcome. It was plain by their exchange of genuine, warm looks that he and Papa were friends. He gazed expectantly at Mama, ready to include her, so that the three so alike in age would lose no time, his time being more precious than ours.

Marcy and I stood side by side holding hands, our intended discreet glances turned bold and free by his manner.

He was a pale young man, so cadaverous that his skeleton seemed covered only with skin. His eye sockets, bone-deep, cupped eyes so glowing, loving, alive that those dark eyes appeared the whole expression of his being. The alabaster of his face and hands said death; his eyes signaled life beyond our experience, making the others in the room nearer death than he.

His name was Fred, the same as one of our horses, which made no difference as our Fred had his own admirable character.

Fred, the man, was very glad to see us all, but he was suddenly and especially glad to meet my sister and me. After the amenities, he asked his father to bring his old wheelchair; he was sitting in a new one.

On her way to the kitchen, his mother said, "I'll make tea."

Mr. Shibley passed us lemon drops in a cut-glass bowl. We received Mama's imperceptible nod of permission and withdrew to enjoy the candy while looking through the lace curtains into the dusty street. Wild gourd vines curled over the dry front yard. No bush or tree grew there; no house, no row of houses obstructed the view of the plain. A few homes and sheds were scattered within the town limits as if the wind had dropped them like seeds. From nowhere a little dust devil whirled into the road, lifting daintily, touching earth again, swaying, dancing. It was a fairy-tale creature of this desolate land, a beautiful thing made of common dust and air, the harmless miniature of the terrible cyclone.

It had picked up a cardboard box along the way and now abandoned it among the gourd vines. Immediately from around the house lumbered a Holstein cow, her black and white hide like a huge map in front of the window. She made for the cardboard box and began to eat it.

Rolling his chair up behind us and pulling back the curtain for a better view, Fred laughed. "Imagine having your lunch delivered by a whirlwind!"

We were fascinated by the cow. She continued to chew and swallow until the box was gone, then moved with no concern for the gourds to the back lot.

Fred dropped the curtain and smiled at us. "She'll break through her fence to get a cardboard box. If you girls ever get one, save it for her."

"Has that stupid Caroline been in the front yard again?" Mrs. Shibley called from the kitchen. "It's a disgrace."

"Oh, I don't know about that," Mr. Shibley said mildly.

"She was—" Fred strained to raise his voice. "Caroline was given a new box."

"Given? How given?"

"Manna."

"You know, of course"—Mrs. Shibley was speaking to the others—"that Holstein cows give a lot of milk, but it is practically skimmed. I wanted Fred to have a Jersey, all that cream and butterfat, or a whiteface. But, no. He bought Caroline with his own money, so he bought her because she was pretty. Isn't that the limit? Then he named her after some character in a book he was reading at the time."

"I named her after Caroline the Great," Fred called.

"*Who's* that?" Mrs. Shibley asked.

"Caroline the Cow, my ruminating friend." Fred laughed softly at his small joke. "Did you girls meet Mr. Tullery at the store? He brings over a box once or twice a week and we have a lot of fun watching Caroline eat it up."

"She gets plenty to eat," Mr. Shibley said.

"She's fey," Papa said, then rounded this off with his logic. "There's something in the cardboard that she needs."

"Let's have tea in the kitchen," Mrs. Shibley invited. "Come, dears."

"May we have ours out here?" Fred asked. "The girls and I?"

His mother brought a tray with slices of warm bread spread thickly with butter and brown sugar and cinnamon; tea for Fred and milk for us. The fragrance of heated cinnamon hung in the air, an influence, a sense of home and foreign places, dissipating whatever shyness we felt.

Fred was tearing up slips of paper; he handed us each one. "I thought we might play streetcar," he said to us, "but we can do that another time. Let's go traveling." He rolled his old wheelchair to a starting point.

"Fred, drink your tea before it gets cold."

"I will. Now, Marcy, do you want to go first? Mother will need more cinnamon after what she put on our bread, so we'll go to Sumatra and Ceylon to get some. Which do you choose, Marcy?"

"Ceylon."

Fred held the old chair as she climbed in.

"When you get there, ask for cinnamon bark, or, if they have any already powdered in a can, bring that." He whispered to me to go ask his mother for a can of cinnamon, then go around through the bedrooms and place it at the destination, the far end of the room, Ceylon.

I felt myself too old for this game, but I liked Fred and his lovely words, and I wished to ride in the wheelchair. When he asked my help, I was freed to play and to be his aide.

He was instructing Marcy about the chair, showing her how to make a safe turnaround. Papa was rather severe about our manners, so I went through the kitchen to get his permission, as this game would certainly include some noise. He nodded, and Mama said in her gentle way, "Not too loud." Mrs. Shibley handed me not one but two cans of cinnamon. "One to take home from Ceylon," she said.

"Tickets, please," Fred demanded of Marcy. "Ready!" He gave the wheelchair a push and Marcy sailed the length of the room, made a safe turn, and stopped in front of a small stand with a starched white doily and an oil lamp on it. I had placed the cinnamon behind the lamp.

Marcy looked back at Fred; he gave her an encouraging gesture, and she asked no one at all, "Is this Ceylon?" No one answered, but she said in a shy voice we could hardly hear, "Then I'd like some powdered cinnamon or cinnamon bark."

"They keep it behind the lamp," Fred said.

Marcy reached for the can and, forgetting her shyness, giggled and clasped the can to her breast, thanked Ceylon, and got back into the chair.

"You'll have to start your carriage yourself this time," Fred said. "Roll the wheels."

Marcy returned from Ceylon, proud to be driving the carriage. She handed the cinnamon to Fred.

"Now," Fred said. "You are clear back in Baca County, Colorado. You must be hungry. There's a café just there where you can get bread and milk. Sit down and enjoy yourself while Cheyenne makes a trip to Sumatra for more cinnamon.

"Cheyenne, you'll have to go to Sumatra. Ceylon is temporarily out of cinnamon. Sumatra is in the Malayan archipelago."

I loved those strange and beautiful words that only Fred knew; the places he was describing to Marcy as I took my own trip to a faraway island. I forgot the house, the wheelchair, the make-believe game, and went to Sumatra and back again to bread and milk at the Colorado café where Fred and Marcy were eating. I handed him the cinnamon, which brought me back to reality.

"We'll take some more trips after tea," he said.

I overheard the parents talking of other states. Papa had spent his youth wandering around and he loved to tell about his adventures and people he had known.

"Fred hasn't been anyplace at all," Mrs. Shibley said, "not even school, but he has some school books and he has read that old geography ragged. He almost makes me believe he's been to some of those queer places."

"Strange places," Mr. Shibley corrected.

"Strange and queer, if you ask me," she retorted.

After our tea, we went for rides to Ceylon, Sumatra, Singapore, and Kuala Lumpur, and other places on the shores of the Java Sea. The fast rides with hairpin turns, our care in dodging furniture, our growing abilities at maneuver made us yell in delight and laugh freely for the first time since we had arrived in our new home.

"I haven't laughed so much in years," Fred said, wiping the perspiration from his pale face. His head, heavy on his weak neck, lolled back in renewing laughter as if it would fall and roll away. His feeble voice released his pleasure in small brave shouts and trembling, determined murmurs.

"It's about time you milk Caroline," Papa said. "We'd better be going. We have to go by Tullery's and pick up our groceries."

During the thanks and the good-byes, Fred's dark eyes were still merry, although his hands left wet marks on the armrests of his chair. "Come next Saturday! Any Saturday! I'm always home. That is"—he turned to Marcy and me—"that is, unless I'm in Makassar."

He joined us to him in these private asides that although spoken aloud seemed a secret among us. We had a friend, we had Fred, who warmed our isolated lives.

We drove home in the dark, such a dark as we had never seen, a black primeval dark, the darkness beyond the sun. The horses knew the way, they plodded slowly along the shallow ruts of the road, as sure of their homing in the night as in the day, their harness sounds making a leathery rhythm soft under the wagon's creaking. The stars were withdrawn, small, giving no light, unlike other nights when they seemed to hang large from the sky ready to be reached for and taken into our hands.

We were all silent within a great silence. The air was sharp, cool. No insects sang. We met no one. Our small company of five persons, two horses, and a dog traveled through the black night as in the infinite black of space.

A huge moon slid up from the eastern rim of earth slowly at first, then swiftly into the sky. We saw the plain, vaster than by day, lost in the mystery of night, reaching far, far, the furry back of an old earth in an ancient time, frightening and beautiful under the sheen of the moon. The sense of an aboriginal time was strong in the nights of the plain.

This moon was not the one I knew, not an ornament of summer evenings, or the reassuring lamp of winter dark. It was a world of liquid light, magnetic, overpowering, rousing in my child's mind a furtive knowledge not yet lost. I was awed; kept silent by a wondering stir of beauty, a longing of spirit asking a first and eternal question of the universe.

Grandfather Alonzo startled me by saying, "Plants need that moon. They soak up the sun all day but they grow in the night. Next spring when we plant, I'll show you. Somehow or other the moon has something to do with growing."

I listened to him waiting for spring. Marcy was asleep. He covered her with a quilt. I wanted to be still and so did he. I wanted to live in the night, the moon's pull, the strange splendor of this vast wild land.

The road ran for a ways along a fenced field; here also were thin, barked telephone poles with a single wire. An owl sat on every post. Their great immobile eyes stared, their heads swiveled. They were watching for prey, the little field mice, no doubt, but to me they were curious, even ominous, an owl on every slender post like a night-blooming flower.

4

AFTER OUR VISIT to Dr. Burtis, Grandfather Alonzo now and then sat peeling a potato as one would an apple, careful to keep the slowly unwinding peel intact. As we were usually on the edge of hunger or actually hungry, this potato was a treat, and his studied peeling of it gave us a ceremony as well. Usually he sat in the barn and usually, not without guile, my sister and I played near the door, around the huge hillock of manure shoveled there, saved to fertilize the fields. When he had finished, he called us, handing us each a fourth of the potato and a short ribbon of peel. He ate the rest solemnly without speaking, wiped his knife first on his trousers and then between two fingers, closed it, and slid it into his pocket.

"In the spring," he said on one of these afternoons, "you girls can pick some young tumbleweeds, pick them when they first come up and look like two soft needles, and we'll eat them. I'll show you where to pick some other greens along the creek."

Often my sister stayed with Papa at whatever he was doing,

and if Mama didn't need my help, that gave me a chance to be alone with Grandfather Alonzo. He was most uncommunicative, and the only gesture of affection he made toward me was a rare small thump of knuckle on my shoulder. This I treasured greatly, especially as it came when I least expected it, giving me long thoughts on its immediate cause; but even when I thought I had discerned the reason, I did not seek its expression because that would take away the sweet delight of its surprise.

One morning I discovered him shaving in the barn. This was unusual, as a small mirror was nailed to the highest point of the dugout entrance and there, every morning of good weather, Papa and he shaved outside. Here he was, standing before a broken bit of mirror fastened to the barn wall. I noted also that his great black overcoat was hanging from a nail behind a stack of bailed alfalfa hay.

"Are you moving to the barn?" I asked, and he jumped, not having heard me come in.

"Not yet," he said significantly and the emphasis was not lost on me. I felt sorry for him and guilty that we had taken over his little one-room home, which for one had been a snug place, but which for five was a packed burrow with no escape tunnels such as even the common rabbit had provided for itself.

"Papa should get a tipi for us." I remembered the Oto tipis and would have preferred one to the dugout.

"It's no mind," Grandfather Alonzo said. "Besides a tipi would never get us through a winter here."

"I've been in a tipi in winter. We had a fire in the middle and smoke went out the top."

"Well, I don't think your mother and father would like that as much as you do."

"I like you better than Papa," I said. "Are you an Indian?"

"No, I am not an Indian, sorry to say, if your liking me depends on that."

"You're the color of an Indian and your eyes and hair are black like theirs."

"Not quite the color," he said. "Did you ever see an Indian with a mustache like mine?"

"No. But why are you not white like Mama and Papa?"

"Irish and Welsh, Spanish-dark from the Armada days, perhaps."

I liked the sound of "Armada days," but I did not ask the meaning for fear it was a dire or disgraceful secret.

"Papa says you have lived alone here for years like a damned hermit."

"Your father is given to kind remarks like that." It seemed to me from this and exchanges between them that Papa and Grandfather did not like each other. Already I knew better than to pursue this subject.

"When you were living alone like a hermit, did you shave every morning like now?"

"Of course."

"Why?"

"To keep my self-respect."

I knew that self-respect was a valuable possession, as Papa mentioned it often in the same breath as pride. Have you no self-respect? Have you no pride? He wasn't worth a dime, he had no self-respect. That sort of thing. This new revelation caused me concern.

"Can I have self-respect without whiskers?"

Grandfather's serious, inward-looking face changed swiftly. He smiled, then he laughed, then he bent over and laughed in a strangled painful way. His long brown hand that held the razor, its ivory handle touched by his little finger, the blade held at a just-so angle for sliding down the skin, mowing the black whiskers in the white soap foam, now waved about as if slashing the air. His laughter would not stop for a long time. He straightened up at last and wiped the tears from his eyes.

"Do you know that if you live here, you will grow up an ignoramus? There is no school within miles."

What did that have to do with whiskers and self-respect?

"Mama and Papa are worried that I cannot go to school," I said, hoping that Papa's concern would give him a better status with Grandfather Alonzo.

"Never mind. Do you want to go to school?"

"Yes."

"Then I will teach you."

"We have no books."

"I have one book. That will do for the time being."

"What book? Will I like it?"

"*The Adventures of Kit Carson.*"

I was silent. I did not know who Kit Carson was, but he had adventures and that made it all right.

"Kit Carson, then," he said, "and the newspapers stuck on my walls." He said this last with bitterness. "You will cut your teeth on murders and scandals, divorces and lawsuits, fires and all the dirty stuff of cities, the dirt of life."

He turned back to finish his shaving and said no more. I left the barn wishing that lessons might never begin. I slid my bare feet along the ground, wanting to know about princesses and castles and witches, and everything growing and struggling to live in this barren and beautiful land.

5

BEFORE WE WERE used to our new life, the men went off to the foothills of the Rocky Mountains for firewood. This annual trek of more than a hundred miles each way was known as "going to the cedars." In a way it was a work holiday for the homesteaders, few as they were in this range country. Several wagons drove in caravan. Once in the forest, the men "camped out" along streams, cooking fish or game over a campfire, eating together, sleeping in the open. They felled trees, sawed them into stove lengths, and drove slowly the long way home, the wagons loaded, the horses pulling hard.

Bounce, the black shepherd dog, with brown spot eyebrows, disconsolate at being separated from Grandfather Alonzo, lay in the sun and slept, rousing himself only to chase a rabbit. The first two days he did not eat at all and was so inconsolable that we gave him more than our usual affection, but this did not prevent his long naps or his slow, tail-down trips to the barbed-wire gate. There he stood looking up the dirt road for long periods, and seeing or hearing no sounds of his friend, he walked back, his body eloquent of grief. He did not try to follow, as he had been told firmly by Grandfather to stay behind and watch over us. By instinct, or from his heritage of generations of herding and protecting sheep and cattle, he understood this and demonstrated it, but we wondered that with his high intelligence he did not also understand that Grandfather Alonzo would return. It may be that he did, that his sorrow was in the waiting, but there could be no doubt about its intensity.

Early in the morning of the second day, we saw a man coming over the plain from the direction of a shack far out on the unfenced range. He moved toward the road and would soon reach it and continue north past our dugout, that is, if he meant to continue. The three of us were in the yard, Mama hanging up clothes that she had washed in the water from the horses' barrel, since it would be stale and undrinkable before they came back. We had never seen the man but, without speaking, we knew who he was, and we were afraid.

In such distant and desolate places, and in new towns where no one knows another, a few come to hide, to forget, to start over again, or as this old man, to take on the protective coloration of an uninhabited land. He had been here before all other settlers, and when they came, he kept to himself. He owned no horse or dog, going on foot the few places he went: to the nearby creek for water and, rarely, to the town for the staples of flour and lard, and perhaps sugar, although one cowboy had seen him taking wild honey from a beehive in a log at the creek. He spoke to no one. If he had, others would have spoken.

A frontier early or late seems to inspire a certain respect for the privacy of others, a tolerant hesitance to question motives and make arrogant judgments, a virtue soon dissipated in towns and even more so in sophisticated places where everyone becomes an expert on everyone's behavior. Perhaps, then, back of that friendly discretion, was the thought that anyone willing to face the hardships of proving up a government claim in that rainless, treeless land deserved the faith and belief accorded the newborn, that he would grow into a man. I am not sure this generous attitude would have been given a questionable lone woman. There were only hard-working wives and daughters. The man walking toward us that morning was solitary and strange, unknown to everyone, and because of this, he was talked about with more interest. At some time or other, someone had heard about his past—not known him, but had known others who had known him.

The secret was out, but it was whispered, not as gossip, but as warning. He was to be let be. That was all. The secret was terrible. It raised the fine hairs on our arms when we heard it, and the sight of him chilled our bodies in the sun. He had no name; the name others called him was Old Loony. His being off in the head was as frightening as what we heard of him, that he was a murderer, that he had murdered his wife, served time in prison, and kept some grisly memento of his crime. A cowboy had actually talked with him once, intending to visit him again more in curiosity than friendliness, but the cowboy had been killed that spring by an enraged bull; and no more was learned of Old Loony.

We watched him, pretending not to. He was a single moving object absurdly small in that immense space under that immense blue sky. We could have gone down the steps into the dugout, but our human fascination with the dangerous and strange kept us in the open, filled with false courage, our muscles tensed to run if need be. For all the space, for all the circumstance of safety, our sense of peril was more acute than it might have been in a crowded place. Our vulnerability stood like a presence among us.

"I want to go inside," Marcy said, "but he could kick the windows in. I wish we lived in a real house." She kept near Mama, walking in and out among the wet clothes on the line, watching Old Loony.

Without saying anything at all, without any pretensions of calm or courage, and I do not know by what quality, except that she was really brave, Mama surrounded us with the atmosphere of her goodwill and gentle pluck.

The old man had reached the road and was now walking toward our fence, three strings of barbed wire on small cedar posts. The gate as well was three loops of wire on a fence post. With frequent mending the fence kept out range cattle and great tumbleweeds.

"I wish Papa was here," Marcy said, and I wished for Grandfather Alonzo.

Only that morning, after the first loneliness, we had awakened feeling glad to be alone, free of the men, released to ourselves.

The authority was lifted; changes simply occurred in our routine. Mama played the piano right after breakfast and sang love songs from her single years. The evening before, she had played and sung hymns and told us stories of her childhood, of Papa's court-ship and the romances of her friends. We knew all those unknown people; their lives had entered our own. We had been in the bed-rooms of the big white house with the giggling girls, Mama among them, secretly pinning ruffles over their young breasts and fastening pads over their slender hips, before Sunday walks or evening parties. We were forever attached to a young man who had killed himself after Mama's sister had broken their engage-ment and married another man. We had watched through Mama's eyes that large group of friends ice-skating in winter and boating in summer or attending band concerts in the flower-fragrant park. We heard our elegant little grandmother exclaim-ing in her soft Southern accent, "Oh, horrors!" at the premature ruffles and pads, at the "wildness" of the young generation. We saw that big white house burn and Grandfather Greenberry sav-ing only the family Bible and the albums of family pictures. We heard of childish fun and young love and broken hearts and big weddings. The three of us had an adventurous evening, late to bed, without the men, up early to more music and singing. We were happy to be free of the men only because they would re-turn; but with the second morning less than half-gone, we wished them home to protect us from this unwelcome and evil stranger.

An even more frightening thought occurred to me: Old Loony, who was almost never seen, had waited until the men had gone, taken the horses, leaving us with no means of escape. We debated for a moment whether we should be safer in the dugout with its two windows flush on the ground, or in the open where we could surely outrun him, although we could see with what strength and steady speed he walked on the road. The idea of enclosure made us feel panicky; we chose to risk the outdoors.

The old man was approaching the gate now and the three of us, hardly able to keep from watching openly, hung up the re-maining clothes, Marcy and I handing them to Mama, all of us waiting to see if Old Loony would walk on toward the town seven miles away. He stopped and looked in our direction. The gate was fifty yards out and we could see his face, but we could not see clearly his eyes and mouth, the two most revealing features.

"Poor man," Mama said in a low voice. "I ought to speak, or offer him a drink of water."

I felt the same. But our fear, slowly accumulated, was slow to give way.

He placed his hand on the gatepost but appeared only to be resting. He continued to look at us across the gray desolation of the yard marked with wagon wheels and horses' shoed hoofs. His hand moved on the post. He stood still, gazing at us with no expression of greeting or expectation on his face. The concentration of his gaze was so set that I could imagine him standing there for days and nights, his unseen eyes binding us to this fearful spot. Such unmoving stance, such silent observation appeared also to presage a sudden action. Was he so lonely that the sight of a woman and two children about their chores gave him a pleasure he could not relinquish? Or was he hostile that still another family had come to these high plains he possessed in a way no legal title gave possession? Whatever his reason, he continued to observe us.

Mama could endure it no longer. She called out over the clothesline, "Good morning!"

Old Loony kept his silence; we thought he nodded but we were not sure.

At this moment, without Old Loony having made one move, Bounce, who had been watching him with no show of alertness, gave a low growl, baring his teeth, but lying still. The old man still made no move, but we felt his eyes now too long upon us. The hair rose slowly along the back of the dog's neck and along his spine; he crouched, his belly just clearing the ground. Thus he crept in a slow, ominous semicircle.

At last the old man walked on toward town. Until Old Loony had passed our fence and was walking on the open plain, Bounce continued to growl. Then he trotted over to us wagging his tail.

6

THE MEN CAME BACK with tales of wild horses that tried to lure the horses to join them.

"They came every night near our camp," Papa told us, "standing in the trees, whinnying and calling our horses. One stallion kept calling our mares. It was strange, not like breeding time, but just as if they wanted them to come live a free life, too. They made all the farm horses restless, even calm old Dip."

"Williams lost a young mare," Grandfather Alonzo said, "but she took to coming back, hanging around near the camp, and he finally lassoed her. All our horses gave her a wide berth for a time, sniffing, rolling their eyes, and snorting a little. Reckon they got a whiff of wild life off her, and for some reason they were afraid."

"They were sure a pretty sight," Papa said, "running together, their manes and tails long and flying. They had a lot of fun, and they looked happy. Makes a man want to live a wild free life in the forest."

"Well," Mama said, "we're living a wild free life on the plains."

Those tales, in variation, and details of the camping-out lasted us through the long, fierce winter, which shut us away from the little outside life we had. That early winter was already gathering in the gray-white northern sky and could be seen from far off. Grandfather and Papa watched that sky day after day and prepared as best they could for an onslaught of cold such as we had never experienced. Grandfather knew those winters and alone he must have feared them, but he spoke of no such fear. Papa loosened the chicken wire on the roof of the stable and laid on more dry cane and broomcorn stalks, replacing the wire, fastening it tight over the stalks against the wind. He mended the north wall of the barn, using every scrap of lumber he could find to give the horses a better shelter. He was fond of animals and liked cleanliness for them as much as for himself, so that he cleaned the barn every morning and enjoyed telling how Grandfather had grown careless alone and had let the barn go; how he, Papa, had shoveled out "enough manure to fertilize a field" the day after his arrival.

To this Grandfather said nothing; he was guilty, and he had to endure hearing the repetition of his offense.

One day Mama said with bitterness, "They are always separating and getting together again. Grandfather lived with us when we were first married, and he's been back and forth half a dozen times since. 'Never again' they said last time; then Alonzo began sending for Walter from this godforsaken place. I can't understand them."

Nevertheless, the coming of winter joined them in common effort; the tasks, the pressure of time, the results to be admired by us all drew forth a comradery they had not shown before. Their good humor, even laughter, came with them down the dugout steps at noon and evening mealtimes. The small room seemed larger, the scant meals more satisfying. Our cramped lives were eased of hidden irritations and our feelings freed to grope toward love. Grandfather told stories of the "early days" and our attention changed his appearance. His dark eyes so sharp and secretive became tender with memories.

"We're living about the same as those early times again," Grandfather said. "How many other Americans are living like old pioneers? Remember these times and you'll have something better in you than the poor city kids."

Papa nodded, but Mama was silent.

"Let's have a song, little girl," Papa said to her. "Play the piano and we'll all sit back and listen. Sing 'Red Wing.'"

As Mama began to play, Papa whispered to us all, "She needs a woman friend. She'll be all right then." Mama's clear lovely voice rose against the silence of the night plain, the silence we could hear as plainly as the music. Her loneliness showed through the pleasure of her singing. At the end she whirled on the stool and smiled at Papa.

"Come here," Grandfather said. He had heard something we had not. "Come to the window."

We went two by two and gazed along the ground.

"Look hard," he urged.

Then, we saw them, a rough semicircle of coyotes sitting on their haunches on the plain inside the fence, four of them.

"Listening to the music," Grandfather said. "Or just curious. Most wild animals just go on about their lives, but coyotes are interested in people. Walk in the open day or night and you'll find a coyote, or several of them, trotting along even with you, not following, keeping his distance. He doesn't make friends, but he'll do you no harm. Remember, he's a wild dog. He kills for food, but only a few criminals among them kill for the pleasure of killing. He's misjudged. I know. I've had plenty of time to watch out here where there are more animals than men, and the coyote is the most interesting of all of them, men included."

The fear on Mama's face slid away into a smile. That did not mean she would become interested in wild animals or the outdoors. Mama was a town person, an indoors person. She would do anything she had to do, and she enjoyed working, but this secluded life was against her nature. She liked people and friends and the busy life of towns. All her life, others came to her with their troubles; she loved to listen, to give her gentle sympathy without advice. It must have been harder than we ever knew for her to be cut off from human contact outside our family.

"Are the coyotes afraid?" she asked.

"Not here. But they soon stay away if they know a rancher is putting out poison or traps. I wouldn't kill an animal without mighty good reason."

I was already interested in all the wild animals, the little prairie dogs living in their big towns, the skunks, badgers, wildcats, and

many more, but now I was genuinely fond of the coyote. This
was another link with Alonzo, to whom I felt truly related. He
and I had no fear of animals and we did not want them to be
afraid of us. We were not foolishly unafraid. Hungry wolves
frightened him. Bulls on the range were a menace. Tarantulas,
centipedes, rattlesnakes, all of which were common, were to be
avoided.

That very night after we had gone to bed with friendly thoughts
of the coyotes, we had a terrifying experience with a huge aggressive rat that had come into the dugout from the fields or the
barn and in the night had bitten one of my big toes. He must have
been exploring, touched my foot, and when I moved, he bit me.
The moving weight of him in the dark frightened me more than
the pain. My shriek brought a quickly lighted lamp and a sicken-
ing hour to follow. The rat remained on the cot and showed fight.
Papa lifted the door into the night, the cool air rushed in, we kept
still to encourage the rat to go his way, but he would not. He
glanced at the open door, lifted and lowered his nose a few times
as if he were sniffing the air in calm leisure, and then resumed his
attitude of anger and attack. I felt paralyzed with fright and
revulsion. He was probably confused and defensive, but his eyes
like glass beads, his teeth revealed by his snarl made him appear
furtive and cruel.

At last Papa reached for a piece of stove wood to drive him out,
and he gave a great leap and ran under the other bed. Papa then
urged him with the broom and he ran to the first step where he
could easily have escaped, but he turned back again, bared his
teeth, and stiffened for fight. It was as if he wished to fight rather
than escape. In that small room we were five persons, all much
larger than the rat weighing several pounds, but his intelligent
angry face showed that he knew he had some mysterious advantage over us all. For dark reasons we did not question, ancient
memories we did not remember, each was absorbed in his own
awareness of the loathsome creature. Yet, he was admirable, and
we must have sensed that too, for we wished him to run up the
steps and back to the fields. Suddenly he leaped down to the
floor, ran and leaped up onto the cot. I sprang away from him
and pressed against the wall. He turned to face Papa again, prepared to resume his fight on the bed.

As suddenly Papa's attitude changed. He was no longer gently urging the rat to its freedom, no longer trying to outwit this clever intruder; he was protecting me. He struck with the piece of cedar firewood, missed, and the rat leaped to the floor and ran to the step, where it seemed he would at last escape; but again he turned and this time he fought, lunging at Papa, dodging his blows, running about the room and back to the steps. A terrible battle went on and on, and because the rat, clearly aware of the doorway, would not leave, he was finally killed with blows. We were all of us worn out, sleepy, sickened with disgust. We felt unclean, as we had felt the rat to be unclean. Mama remembered my toe with its dangerous bite. She washed my foot, covered the wound with raw onion, and bound it in place. Papa went out to throw the rat away. Mama next washed and peeled a potato and gave me the peelings to eat at once.

The night had gone and we had hardly slept. Still we were glad to see the murky light of dawn on the two small windows and floating down the steps like a dirty scarf.

7

PAPA WAS SHOUTING for us to listen. The welcome sound was a long way off, but we heard it and put on our shoes and buttoned our coats over our nightclothes and went up the steps into the gray morning. Papa was washing his hands in the icy cold water beside the dugout. When he finished, he came to us, and we stood in a close group. From far above, melancholy rhythmic cries, barely heard, came down to us. Canadian geese were flying south so high that they were like fine strings dropping their music, their instinctual calling that called to us as well.

"They're a sure sign that winter will soon be here," Papa said.

A radiant white light filled the east and in a moment more the sun, so red and immense that it seemed we could see it burning, slid above the straight horizon, casting long pink rays across a morning-blue sky. We strained our eyes to see the geese, and finally we found them, only their arrowed formations small and fine, far away, thousands of geese migrating south, continuously honking, perhaps to lead those that came after.

Any sounds of travel intensified our sense of isolation. But we were fortunate to live beneath this flyway and to see each spring and fall the great dark flocks of migrating birds.

The geese came from northern Canada, following the Mississippi River valley, fanning out on tributary flyways, on their way to the Gulf of Mexico or sanctuaries in the southern United States. There they grazed and fed and selected their mates. In the spring migrations they flew back to their far-north nesting grounds.

"If we could grow winter wheat here," Papa said with a quiet, private longing in his voice, "those geese might stop here to rest and feed. They fly mostly at night and rest by day in a safe place. It would be a pretty sight to have the fields covered with wild geese. I've seen them, gray backs and black necks. Of course, they need water too, so this is no place for them."

"Wouldn't they eat up all the new wheat?" Mama asked.

"No. They just nip off the green shoots and don't hurt the root. Cattle graze on the new winter wheat the same way."

The arrowed formations came on and on, and we listened again until Papa was moved to tell us more from his odd assortment of knowledge and a good memory.

"Maybe there's one or two hundred thousand geese up there, maybe more, but they're traveling in families, or parts of families, or alone. They mate for life, and if a hunter shoots a mate, or one dies, the other keeps the young geese together with her or him, until they mate. The mate left alone never mates again but keeps on migrating."

"Do they always fly the same way?" I wanted to know.

"Yes. There are different migratory routes, but the same geese fly the same flyways year after year. You should see them when they light. They come down as families and leave as families. Those ganders have got their minds on watching out for their mates and young geese. They all feed, but the ganders are always alert to danger unless they know it's a safe place, and they *know.*"

The cries faded and we could no longer see the penciled sky.

"Well, we'll hear them again in the spring," Grandfather said. "In the fall, their honking sounds sadder than in the spring."

Then we heard another sound, that of a wagon, on the cutoff from the southeast. When it drew near enough that we could see how the two people on the high spring seat were dressed, Mama exclaimed with such rare delight that we all turned to look at her.

"There's a woman on that wagon!" Quick tears she tried to blink away ran down her face.

"A young woman, too," Grandfather Alonzo said. "About your age, maybe twenty-five."

"Oh, glory!" Mama said. "Let's ask them in to rest."

"I wouldn't," he said. "That will be Carrie Mayo Whitehead, and don't forget the Mayo. She's leaving Jim."

Mama appeared heartbroken.

"Happens two or three times a year. They start at dawn and Jim drives her to Lamar, and she gets on the train and goes off in high dudgeon to stay with some of her folks. When she cools off, she comes back and you'd never know she left. Just give her a few weeks and then you two can get together."

The wagon was passing by. The men raised their right hands in greeting, but the woman, dressed in a long coat, her face hidden in a hood, sat erect on the seat looking straight ahead.

"I wouldn't let her come back," Papa said.

"You might," Grandfather said. "That Jim has a fiery temper, and that Carrie has a high spirit."

"I wish I could see her face," Mama said.

8

DURING OUR EVENING VISIT to the cane patch before going to bed, a soft snow was falling. The northern sky was heavy with winter storm. A cold wind rose, shaking the dry cane stalks, and the feathery snow turned to icy barbs and whirled up from the ground and away on the wind. We heard the dugout door rise and drop and Grandfather's long steps going toward the barn.

All night we heard the wind and felt it entering every crack and crevice, strong and freezing cold. It tugged at the dugout's slant door, threatened to break the windows, and lashed over the plain in long sorrowful howls. We woke from our bone-cold sleep at daybreak; the windows were dark.

"A blizzard," Grandfather said. He lighted the oil lamp and with cold stiff fingers built the fire in his penurious way, careful of wood so hard to obtain. From a kindling stick he cut shavings with his pocketknife until a small heap curled in the grate of the monkey stove, its two round lids and the center divider stacked on the iron rim. Over the shavings he laid a patterned network of cedar bark and twigs, and over these a piece of two-inch branch with another in readiness. He struck a match and lighted the shavings, blowing on the flame, fanning it with his long brown hand, directing the fire where he wished. When the flame caught well, he replaced the stove lids and turned the damper to adjust the draught in the black tin chimney that rose up through the roof. The burning made a pleasant small roar in the cold room.

We leaped from our beds and dressed quickly, each in his accustomed space so as not to be in the way of another. When the five of us were in the dugout, there was hardly a foot to spare.

Mama was already preparing the coffee in the granite pot, the coffee that would be warmed over, diluted, extended for days until no further extension was possible. This was a good morning when the coffee was fresh. As we had little else, Marcy and I were given hot water with coffee. We sat at the wooden table covered with oilcloth, our five tin cups and tin plates gleaming in the lamplight. The warmed flour-and-water hardtack occupied the center of the table and gave off a flat odor that nevertheless had its charms for our hunger. We each broke a piece from this pancake and poured over it thick brown sorghum molasses from a white china pitcher Mama had managed to bring along from our other life. That pitcher among the tin was a treasure that between meals rested on the piano and, in spring, held white soapweed blooms or branches of wild sage, and the blue, red, and yellow wild flowers that I always thought of as brave.

Grandfather glanced at the windows now and then, and when no light from dawn or sunup dimmed our lamp, he rose and went to examine the darkened glass.

"Snow," he said. "We're in a drift. Drifted over."

Papa put on his work coat and started up the stone steps.

"Where are you going, son?"

"To see about the horses."

Grandfather shook his head. "We're snowed in," he said quietly.

"Well, what if we are? I have to go to the barn, so I'm going."

"You can try."

Papa was irritated by this patient tone. Bracing himself with his hands against the narrow walls of the entrance, he pressed a

shoulder up against the door, which lay on a slant almost hori-
zontal above his head. The door failed to open or make the
slightest sound of giving. Papa hunched his great strength into
his arched back, braced himself again and pushed. Nothing happened. He picked up a crowbar from among the tools there and
began to pry at the door's edge. Still the door remained fast, and
in his urgency he broke off a splinter of wood.

"Careful," Grandfather said with infinite calm.

"Careful, hell!" Papa glared at his father. "What are you going
to do, stay in here all day?"

"We may. I have. Sometimes more than a day or two. I lost
count."

"What about the horses?" Papa was more alarmed about the
horses than about ourselves.

"They were snowed in too."

"They could have died of thirst for all you cared."

"Well, a little snow drifted in and they ate that. Better off than
I was. I finally broke a window pane and got some snow for myself, but it was gloomy with the window boarded up till I got to
town. That was some time."

"They must have been knee-deep in dung."

"They were."

"I suppose you were too."

"Well, now, we needn't discuss that."

"It's a fact we'll have to put up with if we can't get out. What
do you say to that?"

"We can dig a hole in the floor—it's dirt—and take the soil out
later and replace it with clean dirt."

Grandfather's calm reasoning, his voice of experience infuriated
Papa. Our fastidiousness, already having suffered so many blows,
was once more to be assailed. Mama appeared resigned to anything, but beneath her quiet mask something was stirring to
emerge at a future time when we had forgotten this latest trial.

"I can't stay in this goddamned hole-in-the-ground all day!"
Papa said as he came down the steps.

"Mama has to—lots," I said.

"Shut up," Papa told me.

"What shall we do?" Marcy asked in a frightened way and
lunged from her perch on the bed into Papa's arms.

"We'll do something," he soothed her. "Your dad will take care of everything. Now, get down, Marcy, get under the covers and keep warm. I want to think."

"What do you suppose has happened to Bounce?" I too was concerned about the animals.

"He's in the barn with the horses. He's all right," Grandfather said. He put another piece of wood in the fire. "I brought this bridle in last night, so I may as well mend it now." He sat down on his cot and began to work on the worn leather.

"Well, I'll be damned," Papa said in amazement.

"We will have to wait for the sun to come out, hoping it will, and it may loosen the snow. Depends on how deep it is."

"What if it turns cold and freezes?" Papa demanded.

"We'll cross that bridge when we get to it."

"Well, I hope we get to it," Papa said meanly. "I want to see you get out of that one."

"I don't know any more than you do," Grandfather said rather sharply now. "But I'm trying to keep calm. Your temper hasn't opened the door yet."

That set Papa to new attempts to raise the door, but when he failed, he hunted up an old deck of cards and began to play solitaire on the kitchen table, apparently absorbed in the game, but it was clear to us that he was mapping a new strategy to defeat this powerful natural enemy.

"This snow will be good for the soil," Grandfather Alonzo said, "good for the soil and the buffalo grass."

Papa smacked his deck down on the table and swept all the cards together. "What the hell's happening to all those poor cattle out on the range, thousands of them?"

"By Jupiter! If you don't think of everything!" Grandfather looked at him and his eyes were black and fiery. He turned back to his harness-mending and said as if he had forgotten his flare at his son, "I feel right sorry for all those cattle; they can't get at the grass. If the men can get out, they'll scatter some cottonseed cake or hay; if they can't . . . well, maybe this won't last. The cattle are much worse off in a blizzard when the zero wind blows and freezes them."

We were used to the silence of the plains, but this snowed-in silence had a different quality. We got through the first day well enough and went to sleep hopeful of the next day's sun. Our lamp had burned all day against the darkness in the dugout, and Mama filled its glass bowl with coal oil in the evening while I shined the glass chimney with old newspaper. Filling and cleaning the lamp was a pleasant little task of every evening, but this day had not the character of others. We did not know whether the snow had ceased or whether it fell and buried us more deeply; but we were glad not to hear the wind.

The second day was more difficult. The men were used to being outdoors, and we were so crowded living every detail of our lives together that nothing mattered more now than our freedom from this tiny underground room.

On the second and third days and nights we heard the cattle bawling, a forlorn and desolated sound, a genuine lament painful to hear. They were hungry and their grass, the short gray curled grass of the high plains, was far beneath the snow, or they would have pawed down to a slight feeding at least. We felt the increased chill through the walls and knew that in spite of their heavier winter coats the cattle were cold.

We stayed in bed wearing our warmest clothing and burned as little wood as possible, but on the third day our wood gave out. That same afternoon we heard small crackling sounds in the snow and we knew the sun was shining, had been shining perhaps all day. Papa began to work at raising the door, and after two hours of trying all the ways he had thought of during those dark days, he managed to raise the door and prop it up enough to crawl through. There was no place to go except into the snow. He gathered his strength and plunged upward like a swimmer battling for the surface. We heard a loud blow of breath and a shout of honest delight.

"Say! It's deep! I've got my head out. The world is sure a pretty sight." He flailed about making a larger passage and called back, "Hand me up the shovel, Dad."

Grandfather pushed the shovel through the loosened snow already caved in over Papa's tunnel, and we soon heard the spirited whoosh and shush of digging.

"I can't get a swing on this," he shouted.

After a long while Papa had pitched enough snow above his head and trampled and packed enough down around him for Grandfather to crawl out with another shovel. When they had succeeded in opening a space for themselves to work, they were not long in uncovering the door. But they were a long time cutting a narrow path between five-foot walls of snow to the barn.

Mama, Marcy, and I came out. Walking in the white corridor was a new delight. In order to see our winter world we must find the woodpile and climb to its top. There we turned slowly around looking over the great circle of snow that for us began with our farm at the center and reached to the horizon. How tell its beauty? It lay white and silent, sparkling in the sun. We stood in awe of the purity laid upon the world giving respite from all that was not in harmony with the deepest yearnings of our souls. Over the earth lay this purest of days, its gentle beauty speaking to a part of us unspoken to, ignored by the hard land beneath.

We must take advantage of the light, so we climbed down and pulled out logs and carried them back to the dugout. None of us wished to enter that underground room until we were forced by the ending day. We followed the men to the barn.

An overhang on the east side made it easy to get in. There, with the patient acceptance of work animals, the horses were in their stalls, hungry but safe. A leak of snow had provided their water. Grandfather led them outside, where they snorted and stamped about in the limited space free of deep snow while Papa cleaned away the manure and filled their mangers with fodder and heads of feterita from the small granary attached to the north side of the barn. Our warm breath made clouds in the cold air, and a small fog rose from the great warm bodies of the horses.

When they were led back into the clean, good-smelling barn, Grandfather curried Dip and I curried Fred, my favorite, a large white horse with dappled hindquarters and a long white tail. His head was less handsome than Dip's, Dip being a big well-bred bay. Fred's wild pink eyes looked at me with trust, and when I laid my cheek against the enormous flat bone of his jaw and spoke to him, he swung his head around with care not to knock me off the stool on which I had to stand in order to curry his back, and nibbled at my arm with soft lips. Fred had under his skin on each shoulder a coin, the size of a quarter, placed there by someone who owned him before Grandfather, and for what reason we could not understand. A superstition, perhaps, or a crude joke of sorts. The skin must have been slit, the coins inserted, and the flesh healed over. These spots were not painful so they remained only a curiosity, but curiosity they were, a mark of man.

I touched one and Fred quivered his flesh as if to dislodge a fly. Then he shook his great head, his coarse mane striking against my face, a sign of tolerant impatience. I held his mane and swung up onto his back, moving about there as on a private continent, currying him, bringing him back to this comforting pleasure.

When we left the barn, we saw Bounce trying to run on top of the snow, hopeful of chasing a jackrabbit for his hunger, but he sank through the snow's soft crust time and again until he realized the uselessness of his efforts and returned sheepishly to the tunneled path. Mama brought him a piece of hardtack and he shared our common food.

Out on the range we could see the dark patterns on the snow— the herds of cattle pressed close together for warmth and protection against the gray wolves who in desperate hunger would attack a stray beast. Then seeing that the snow had blown deeper around the farm buildings than in the clear, we plunged into a journey to the gate, just to be going someplace, anyplace after the confinement indoors. At each step we were sinking into the snow, rising, lifting our legs for another step, falling, laughing, falling again. Bounce floundered about, joyous for our company and the sense of play.

But at the fence our laughter ceased, for there frozen stiff, caught in the barbed wire fence, were three dead steers who had strayed from the herd in the storm. We stared in fascination at this close sight and alien presence of death.

"Coyotes will clear them away," Grandfather Alonzo said, leading us back toward the dugout.

"Clear them away?" I asked.

"Eat them, child. Coyotes keep the plains clean, even if they do catch a few chickens now and then."

"But we have no chickens."

"In the spring we will," Papa said.

"Coyotes catch mostly prairie dogs, anyway," Grandfather said, "rabbits and rats. All great breeders; coyotes keep them down."

"You talk as if the coyotes are personal friends of yours," Papa said.

"Well, when you live here alone as long as I have, they'll be your friends too. I listen for them to yip and bark and sing, and I like to see them sitting around on their haunches looking at me in plain curiosity. They'll bear studying."

"No sheep rancher would listen to such talk," Papa said. "They kill too many lambs."

"Sick ones, maybe. Besides, we have no sheep ranches around here, thank God," Grandfather said. "Sheep ruin the pasture, eating down to the roots and cutting the rest with their sharp hoofs."

"Hell, I like all kinds of animals," Papa said, apparently irritated at somehow having got on the side opposing himself. "But a man living in the wilds has to protect himself from them."

"I'd say it is mostly the other way around," Grandfather said. "The Indians killed buffalo for food and hide and still the plains were black with them, millions of them. The white man slaughtered them all in just a few years. Goddang it, they're after the coyote now, poisoning, trapping, shooting. The wild horses are mostly gone already, hid out in the mountains. What's wrong with man that he can't think in a pattern? Everything has a purpose."

"Now, I'd like to break me a wild horse—" Papa said as if dreaming of this feat. "Break him to ride without breaking his spirit."

"That's the only true way," Grandfather agreed. "Listen—"

We heard the far-off wagon, its small sounds made smaller by our snow-softened world. Then we saw the wagon moving slowly along the road from the big ranch to the south. Cowboys riding to the rear came alongside and were handed sacks of cottonseed cakes. The cowboys rode off across the range to a herd of cattle, their horses plunging and struggling through the snow. Our hearts rose again from the frozen beasts tangled in our fence, from the slaughtered buffalo and the hunted coyote, to the sight of the surviving, living cattle being fed after days of hunger and cold.

Papa was looking at the dead ones in a thoughtful way, no longer interested in anything else. Then he turned on us as if he were angry. "I'm going to take one of those steers. We're just as hungry as the coyotes."

"Steal?" I whispered.

"Shut up! And don't let me ever hear you say a word about this, or I'll tan your bottom."

I knew he would; the experience was familiar. I remembered the first time well, when I had stolen a packet of flower seeds and, believing in magic, was certain that the beautiful colored blooms pictured could be shaken out of the envelope. The results were quite different. First, a spanking; next, a brief explanation of stealing, and last, the humiliation of returning the packet, telling the storekeeper I had stolen it, which was wrong, and that I was sorry. I determined never to steal again.

"But it's *stealing*." I dared to correct Papa as he had corrected me.

At times he spoke to me as an equal. "Now, listen here. These steers are no use to anybody now."

"Maybe their hides," Grandfather said.

"Damn it all! Stay out of this!"

"This is still my farm, son, and I don't want a stolen animal on it."

Papa walked away and came right back. "I'm not stealing! Will the coyotes be stealing?"

"I can't say they will be; no."

"After dark tonight we'll come out here and drag one of these steers in and I'll saw off some meat. We'll get a few square meals. When the weather starts thawing, we'll bury the rest."

"Best get out of sight then," Grandfather said, "so's not to attract the men up here looking for strays."

We went back to the dugout in an atmosphere of conspiracy. All the pure delight of our trip to the gate was gone. Only Marcy still played in the drifts.

"It's going to snow again tonight," Papa said, pointing to the gray northern sky. "The air is getting warmer. Snow will cover up our tracks when we drag him in."

Even the snow was in league with our covert doings.

9

PAPA WENT INTO the dugout first. He was whistling. Grandfather looked at Mama, making that quick sidewise motion of his head that we knew meant disapproval. "Whistling! Beats all!"

"Walt wouldn't ever do a thing like that if we weren't so darned hungry. You know that. The kids look like sticks. They're hungry all the time."

"Now, now, Ginny, don't rile yourself up."

"Well, it hurts me to look at them." She started running toward the dugout and soon fell into the deep snow. She lay without trying to get up and we heard her crying. "Stealing!"

"What's the matter with Mama?" Marcy asked.

"Nothing!" Mama said, getting up and plunging steadily ahead.

"It's being cooped up so long," Grandfather explained.

"Papa didn't cry," Marcy said. "And I don't cry."

"It's no sin, Marcy. It does us good now and then."

"Did you ever cry?"

"When your grandmother died years ago. I can't say I've cried since then."

"Papa said you were just an old drunkard."

Grandfather made a clucking sound with his tongue. He did not look down at Marcy but far away over the snow. "Well, Marcy, that's right. I was for a time, but that's all over long ago."

"Why?"

"Why? Why, it didn't bring her back. That's why."

"Did you think she'd come back?"

"No, child, I didn't. That was the trouble."

"What is a drunkard?"

"Well, now—"

"It's bad, isn't it?"

"Well, you see—"

"Dad! Hey, Dad! Come on back here and help me fix this floor. We've all got to get this damn place clean before dark."

Grandfather looked down at Marcy. "Excuse your grandpa now. We'll talk another time, or you can ask your father."

"You don't like Grandfather," I accused her. "Why?"

"Because he is not the same as Papa."

"Of course not, silly."

"You like him." She came close to me and pinched me hard, twisting the skin. "I don't like anybody but Papa."

I made a snowball.

"What is a drunkard?" she asked me.

I knew and I didn't know. I had seen men drunk and fighting in the street; I had seen them drunk, staggering and singing. Once I had seen a drunk man sitting on the boardwalk crying and I had felt sorry for him. I remembered our Indian friend with his eyebrows shaved off, flashing his hunting knife.

"I don't know."

"You know and you won't tell me," Marcy said and pinched my arm again.

I threw the snowball. She came at me with her head down and butted me in the stomach. I went down, but I was up at once. I pushed her hard. It was a safe fight because we were falling into the deep snow. We fought angrily for a few minutes, then separated and began to pelt each other with snowballs. Bounce ran from one to the other barking, enjoying our angry game.

Papa came up the steps and shouted back to Mama. "The kids are having fun; they're in a snowball fight."

We had to pretend. When we were struck, we each fell back

into the snow and lay still. In that stillness we heard the wagon coming and leaped up. Papa's face changed in an instant and the energy went out of him.

"There goes the meat," he said dully.

Grandfather was looking at the men on the wagon. "It's Banter and two of his sons. Why don't you ask him if you can buy one of the steers."

"With what?"

"He'd probably give you the carcass for skinning it. It may be a day or two before they pick up the frozen strays, anyway."

Papa's face woke up into anger. He carried the shovelful of soiled earth far away from the dugout, threw it into the snow, and came back as fast as he could, lifting each leg high and ramming it down hard as if he were tramping on his humiliation. He stopped in front of Grandfather. "You think I have no more pride than that?"

"More than your share likely."

"Well, it keeps me going in a place like this."

"You came out here of your own accord, son."

"After those flowery letters. The 'last chance to pioneer.'"

"That's right. So it may be. I thought you'd like the adventure. My father and his father before him cleared the wilderness and made their homes. You used to like to hear your granddad tell about those old days. It will be a good life for the little girls."

"If they live through it. And it's hell on Ginny."

"I'm sorry about that. I thought you'd have your own place, remember. It didn't turn out that way and we'll make the best of it."

"I don't want to make the best of it," Papa said. "I don't mind to work hard but I want to make a living at it."

"We'll plant in the spring. We'll have crops."

"It's too dry here."

Grandfather smiled and waved his arm at the snow. "Someday they'll raise winter wheat here."

"Someday, always someday."

"Well, there they are. I'm going out to the road to ask Banter about his cattle."

"I'll go along to see you don't ask any favors."

"Come along."

"It'll be damned good to talk to someone," Papa said and began to smile. "Maybe pick up a little news." He raised his arm and waved at the Banters and they waved back.

Our anger forgotten, Marcy and I moved closer to the dugout and Mama. What is pride? I wondered.

IO

How GOOD IT WAS to live in a clean, fresh room again! Mama melted snow and washed all our clothes. They froze into stiff shapes on the line and we carried them in like so many boards. She struggled up the steps with heavy bedding. The strong freezing wind, sweeping the snow off the plains, flapped the bedding so violently that one of the cedar posts supporting the wire was broken and had to be replaced from the woodpile. Mama's hands were red and numb with cold, and the next day the skin on her knuckles broke and bled.

"But we're clean again," she said to Marcy and me. Then, "No matter how hungry you get, don't mention meat before your dad. We'll manage. Many people never eat meat. Do you understand?"

We understood.

Papa reluctantly traded his ruby stickpin to a young man in town for some secondhand lumber and a little cash with which he bought shingles and nails and basic food supplies. For the next few days he and Grandfather worked fast to build what was called a "doghouse," a small upright entrance to the dugout. We might be snowed in again, but our slant door would not be covered and imprison us. Grandfather made a new bench that was placed against one outside wall of the doghouse. In summer a pail of water would stand at one end with a dipper hanging above it on a nail. Two washpans hung on the wall for the men to use morning and evening. Grandfather secured a piece of broken mirror at their tall eye level. Mama's washtub and boiler were hung on the other side of the doghouse.

Indoors, aside from the flour and lard in the two big cans used for chairs, our sparse food supply arrayed on the shelves greeted us as we went up and down the steps: salt, sugar, salt pork, coffee beans, a treasured can of tomatoes, and a gunnysack of pinto beans. We could buy no more but at least our diet varied from hardtack to pintos. The fragrance of pinto beans bubbling on the little monkey stove all day added immeasurably to a sense of home and, even, comfort. There were times to come when we had none of these foods and returned to our hardtack; there were times when Papa was lucky enough to shoot a jackrabbit, lucky enough to get one without blisters. There was a time to come seven days long when we had no food at all. But that was not now; now was better because of Papa's tiepin. He still had his gold watch, inherited from his grandfather, and nothing we could imagine would make him part with it, nor did we wish him ever to do so. It was the same with Mama's wide gold wedding ring. However poor we became, however much we failed, we did not even consider these possessions as anything to be sold or bartered. Not in those first years.

The Christmas and New Year holidays were the most unusual we had known. In other years we were used to the traditional turkey dinner, pies, fruitcakes, a decorated, candle-lighted tree, relatives and friends, and for Marcy and me, all day with cousins, sledding in the snow or playing indoors with new toys. The familiar pre-Christmas secrecy pervaded our dugout, and several times Grandfather locked the barn door against us. The town post office yielded not one package and not one letter, but the trip—as all trips to Two Buttes—meant a happy visit with Fred Shibley and those reckless travels in his old wheelchair. He thumbed through his grade school geography, its pages worn soft, its corners threadbare, and with each visit he sent us to foreign places with magical names, such as Samarkand to see the tomb of Tamerlane. Just to see Fred with his eyes glowing in his pale face was a gift for all seasons. He panted and perspired and once nearly fell from his chair, but he created a time of enchantment.

Marcy and I took him a present to be opened on Christmas, but he opened it at once. "I may be in Makassar on the Island of Celebes," he said. Makassar must have been his favorite word; he went there often. We had made him a small flag of our own free design by sticking the points of varicolored grains of Indian corn into an oblong of cardboard. He was delighted. "It is a flag of the world! Just the thing for me!" He lowered his voice and spoke very seriously to us. "Do you know, little friends, that I have never been anyplace but right here?" He knocked lightly on our heads. "Come in!" he called out in a tone of welcome. "You see, you must keep the door open. Your mind is better than a thousand legs, but it is no good with the door closed."

In some way, without questions, I understood what he meant, and perhaps Marcy did too. Fred spoke to us as clearly as wild flowers and rocks and running water and wind spoke to our childish minds; we were one and the same, yet different. We could see the flowers and rocks and water, but we could not see the wind; yet all had their voices, as Fred had his.

He gave us a miniature gunnysack of pecan nuts. I had hoped for one of his books, but Fred had observed our bodies grow thin and our hair like dry grass. "Those pecans are from Mississippi." The word *Mississippi* said with his relish for names was as stirring as Zanzibar.

A few days before Christmas, Grandfather opened the doghouse door and called down into the dugout. "Ginny! Carrie Mayo Whitehead has come home again, and she and Jim are turning in our gate! Better two-step up here and give her a neighborly welcome."

Mama smoothed her hair quickly, glanced in the small mirror on the wall, bit her lips to make them pink, and tied a long clean apron around her waist. She ran up the steps and pushed out the the door so eagerly she nearly struck Grandfather. He smiled.

"Good glory!" Mama said. "Oh, good glory!"

"Wonder if you'll take to each other?"

"Whoa!" Jim Whitehead called out to his sleek team of horses. He smiled like a man renewed. "Howdy, Alonzo."

Carrie stepped on the wagon wheel and leaped to the ground, her long full coat billowing out in the wind. Her brown eyes laughed with her quick smile; she was all softly rounded and spirited. Mama walked to meet her and Carrie said, "Well, I declare, Ginny Babb!" She sparkled for Grandfather. "Merry Christmas, Alonzo. Alonzo, I've had a grand trip."

"Wouldn't be surprised," he said, and Jim laughed.

Carrie turned back to Mama, who was looking at her with pleasure and appreciation. "You'll never know how glad I am to meet you."

"Oh, yes, I do. This is the lonesomest place. I've been to see my family in Denver."

"Won't you come in and have some coffee?"

"No thanks, for today. Jim has to get back to work and I've had a long trip. But we've brought you some packages. When we went to the post office, Mr. Hastings asked us to drop your mail by; he was afraid you'd miss your Christmas gifts and letters from home."

How happy we were to see the packages. Mama thanked Carrie and Jim and added, "I'll thank Mr. Hastings when we go in again."

Carrie came nearer Mama and said in a low, sincere voice, "Ginny, we're going to be friends."

"I know it, Carrie. I knew it before."

"It's a long ways, so all of you must come for a whole day, any Sunday."

"We live here like sardines," Mama said, "but you are both welcome."

Jim and Grandfather had drifted off to the barn to talk with Papa, and Carrie called Jim back and they were gone, but it was plain that Mama's whole world had changed.

On Christmas morning Marcy and I woke to see our long white Christmas stockings nailed to the windowsill, and they were not empty. They were not stuffed full as in other years, but the contents were far more enjoyed. In mine was a wanted and needed pencil, in Marcy's a small pair of scissors with rounded tips: she liked to cut paper. Next were cylindrical boxes made by

Grandfather containing two sets of jackstraws, each stick and spear carved and tinted in one of several colors by him. In the foot of each stocking were an orange and an apple. We were richly gifted! Grandma Greenberry had made a fruitcake, its brandied fragrance overpowering that of the pinto beans. She had sent long woolen underwear for us all, and little silk bags filled with dried rose petals from her garden. Cousins and friends had sewn for Mama small lacy things that no longer fitted into her life but nevertheless added a festive note to what Papa called "a slim Christmas."

When we went to the barn to let the horses out, Papa gave them an extra portion.

"They don't know one day from another," Mama said, laughing and teasing him. He was cleaning the barn.

"But we do," Grandfather said, and from a cold hiding place he brought out a bone for Bounce. We stared at it in surprise and kept silent. Grandfather admitted that he had hacked off a piece of a leg from one of the frozen steers caught in our fence. Bounce ran with it, rolled on it, chewed awhile, and buried it in the softer ground of the cane patch.

"It isn't ready yet," Grandfather said, trying to conceal his embarrassment. "He'll dig it up in a week or two." He went to the horses' water barrels and broke the thick ice; carried water into the dugout from the house barrel, gathered wood.

A long smooth wind came over the plain, so cold that we should have gone indoors as soon as our morning chores were finished, but we lingered, turning, as we often did, to gaze over the flat distance to the far, far horizon, as a man might look over the sea. We stood about, all of us, feeling we must stay close together this holy day. There was no talk of religion. In towns, Mama attended church, but Papa did not. Whatever Grandfather was thinking he kept to himself. But the day was different, even in that empty wilderness, as if the wind that blew was the wind of the world singing a dream, a brave, tireless dream of love and goodwill to men.

In the late afternoon we felt restless. Marcy sat on the bed cutting a sheet of newspaper into ribbons, lost in her childhood fantasies. We had all played jackstraws for an hour, as we were to play it many winter evenings, trying our skill with the tiny spears at raising and removing sticks from a closely intermingled pile.

"Let's sing some Christmas carols," Papa suggested, although he only listened as he "couldn't carry a tune." "Come on, Dad. Cheyenne. Let's have some life around here. Ginny! Play the piano and sing. Sing 'Silent Night' and then something merry."

Mama obeyed with pleasure. She had been admiring a gift box of stationery, eager to write letters. She had said she wished she could do her mending and patching, but she had been taught not to do profitable work on Sundays and Christmas, and she kept to her ways. She arranged herself at the piano, smiled at us all, rubbed her chilly hands together and placed them on the keys, just touching them with affection. She rubbed her hands again, tried her voice, then began to play and sing. No music came from the piano. The keys went down with a plop. She rippled the keys up and down the keyboard, making only flat sounds of ivory, felt, wood. She kept trying, unable to believe this new calamity.

"The snow, the snow that sifted in during the blizzard! And all the dampness!" She started to swing around, then swung back, facing the piano.

"Well, I'll be damned," Papa said.

Mama began to sing the song in her clear soprano, but we were so startled by the silent piano that we forgot our voices. We all knew when she turned we would see the tears on her cheeks; we knew what the piano meant to her. The piano was a wonderful friend to us all. Mama finished the song and got up quickly. Her face was dry.

"Time to clean the chimney and fill the lamp," she said to me.

No one spoke. We were thinking of the confining winter ahead without music, but we were thinking mostly of Mama's composure. Sensitive and easily hurt as she was, she had finally learned to put on a mask.

I prepared the lamp in a hurry to chase the dusk.

"Well, how about 'Jingle Bells'?" Papa said. "The girls would like it."

"Speak for yourself," Mama said, and began to sing. Grandfather gave me an affectionate rap on the shoulder, and we joined her. Even Marcy could sing that.

When the gay little song came to an end, we heard the gray wolves howling so near that Mama shivered, and Grandfather went up the steps and let Bounce in.

II

MAMA AND Papa were concerned that there was no school within a hundred miles, but it was Grandfather who set about teaching me what he could. Several evenings a week we had classes, other nights being kept free so that "school" did not overwhelm our crowded life where no one could escape even for a moment into a private corner, except, as Grandfather said, "into the private corners of our minds." At times, the classes were shifted without notice, depending upon the atmosphere of the dugout. Winter kept us in and moods collided, tempers erupted, tears started, long fermenting silences bruised the air. We walked on eggs. We went to bed even before it grew dark, and we got up at dawn, usually, to find that peace was restored.

"Oh, anything for peace!" Mama said often, her own peaceful nature affronted by the noise and charge of heated words, affronted even by the exciting disagreements of discussion. Although they were different in all other ways, neither Mama nor Grandfather initiated quarrels, and once involved against their wills, they responded with a few mild exclamations such as "Oh, blame it!" from Mama and "Goddang my wildcats!" from Grandfather, spoken in a low, impatient tone meant to end the argument. Their closed faces at such moments suggested the reluctant storing up of umbrage. Papa's powerful energy and spirited nature demanded room and strong expression; the frustration his mistakes had created drove him to angry outbursts and formidable declarations of his will over us. It was I who challenged him, even as a child, causing his furies to soar. Behind my back he boasted of my spirit, but in the fray he was my enemy and I was his. Marcy's contribution at these times was to frown her baby face at us all, and run into the circumference of Papa's wrath, clinging to him in assurance that he would protect her from all the world.

If the day was bright, or if the little room was bursting with our animosities, Grandfather moved our schoolroom to the barn. There he taught me how to handle a knife, or bridle a horse, or distinguish grains, or he read to me from his only book, *Kit Carson.* The author, his name unknown to me, gave us years of pleasure, a sense of the early American Southwest, the excitement of adventure, and a suggestion of the white man's unjust treatment of the Indian. The book gave me also my first formal source of education. I studied it to learn words; I copied from it to learn to spell; I read it to myself and aloud; I copied numbers from its pages; I wrote lessons on what I had read. We wore that book out.

"It ought rightly to be the Bible, if we have only one book," Grandfather said once. "All my people were educated from the Bible by their mothers. They were well-spoken people because of it. By the time they went to school, they had some learning. It was the same with your father and me. His grandmothers looked after that."

"Why don't we have a Bible, then?"

"Your father and I were nonbelievers, or so we imagined ourselves to be. Once, when I was a Socialist, I threw my Bible away. I was afire with Socialism; you won't understand that now. I thought they had the answers to all the injustice of the world, but of course no one has. I'll not forget that day."

"What day?"

"Well, I was moving on. I was just a young fellow, and in those days we walked anyplace we wanted to go, hundreds of miles. I'd just strike out and walk, alone or with a friend. Sleep out, cook our meals on a campfire. Lots of timber then and fine grass. And wild flowers! Birds, wild animals. Not many people. If you wanted a home or a farm, you had to clear the timber and dig up the stumps. I've dug many a stump to make a field."

By now I was interested in the countryside he was describing, but Grandfather came back to *that* day.

"That day I was giving away the things I had accumulated, and when I came to my Bible I'd always carried with me, I threw it out, without offering it to anyone. One of the older men turned pale as a ghost right before my eyes. 'There'll be a curse on ye, made by your own hands,' he said, and picked up the Bible. He handed it to me but I wouldn't take it. Some of my new Socialist friends were there and I wanted to show I was a strong fellow. But it got into my mind and kind of scared me. 'It's a sacred Book,' the man said. 'But it isn't just the Book I mean. It's God. You can't throw God away, he's in your hand still, and your hand is in God. Everything is God!' " Grandfather quit talking and looked away into his memories. After awhile he said, "One of my friends told me, 'Don't pay him any mind, Alonzo; he don't sound like any Christian.' But, it beats all, I never quite forgot him. I went on my way and I said to myself, 'I'll put his words out of my mind.' Well, that's why I have no Bible."

I enjoyed all his stories, and almost anything I asked him prompted a story, if we were alone.

"Your mother must have a Bible somewhere," he said, "but unlikely she'll expose it, not being sure of your father's thoughts on the matter. He wrote her to get rid of everything, and she stood up to him and brought the piano. It may be someday we'll have enough money to get the piano fixed."

Without a Bible, with only Kit Carson, Indian Scout, we sometimes needed a change. Indoors, Grandfather selected short pieces for me to read from the *Denver Post* pasted on the walls. Others he ignored, which meant he forbade, but I read them when he was not around. I was fascinated by all the pieces in the newspaper; each showed me a facet of the world beyond that far circle of horizon. Everything existed out there and I would someday find it. The preponderance of murders, robberies, beaten children, political skulduggery, people in trouble, the evils of the fence law,

the evils of free range: None of these could deter my interest or
my education, mostly because the meaning of all such news was
little understood by me. And so I quickly learned to read.

Grandfather said, "You have your own pattern just like any
one seed. Perhaps you can withstand this blight."

"It's tough out in the world," Papa warned, as if we lived inside the earth, or, as I suspected, within a great circle unrelated to
the world.

"That's exactly right," Mama said, when I asked if this were
true. "It's only hard here."

"Did Kit Carson live this side of the sky or outside?"

"Kit Carson," Papa said, as if he were a fellow student, "was
born in Kentucky, same as your mother, but in 1809. Your mother
was born eighty years later. He was a saddler's apprentice in
Missouri, but when he was seventeen, he joined a caravan and
went to Santa Fe, New Mexico. On the way he saved a man's life.
This fellow had gangrene in his wounded arm, and Kit cut it off
and fixed it up with some wild herbs. He turned into one of the
best scouts, knew the long trails like I know the back of my hand.
He killed an Indian, maybe more, but he turned out to be an
Indian agent, a sympathetic one. Finally married a close relation
of the governor, a beautiful Spanish girl, brought him a big
dowry."

"He fought a duel, too," I said, "over an Indian girl."

"That was Waa-nibe, an Arapaho, when he was young."

"They got married in the Indian way," I said, trying to keep up
with Papa's knowledge about the hero of my studies. "And they
had a little girl."

"Waa-nibe died," Papa said. "Poor woman."

"He was in the Civil War," Grandfather said. "In the Union
Army, a colonel. I was nearly in that war but I was too young. We
hid some slaves though, my people did. Kansas was a Free State.
My people had come out from Virginia, but we were on the side
of the North by then, all of us against slavery."

"Kit Carson married another Indian," I said, "and her name
was Making-Out-The-Road."

"She was a Cheyenne," Papa said. "You know, that's a funny
story. Old Kit was good-natured with women, and she just about
spent everything he had. When he tried to talk to her about it,
kindly too, she settled that marriage right then and there like

any self-respecting Indian woman. She threw all his belongings
outside the lodge. That was the end of it."

"Maybe we could work in a little history," Grandfather said
in his wry way, and we tried. It was difficult.

Both Papa and Grandfather had good minds although un-
trained by formal standards. All their lives they read and "studied"
about things, meaning they thought seriously about them. "I can
size up people," Papa said, and he could. He had a remarkable
and accurate memory, and a vast assortment of facts, but they
were always warmed by his liking for people. Among the assortment was his knowledge of American Indian tribes, especially the
Plains Indians.

Grandfather owned a thick tablet, many of its aging yellowed
sheets covered with his spidery drawings of horses, birds, and
plants. In this tablet he was making long lists of words in a
spidery handwriting that resembled the drawings. The spelling
lessons became a family game, since Papa was proud of his ability
to spell and kept interrupting with words I did not know. Grandfather then made several lists, of very simple words for Marcy,
general ones for me, and hard ones for Mama and Papa. These
spelling bees were a source of fun and laughter and sometimes
hurt feelings, as Papa must win over Mama, often by bringing in
difficult Indian names, such as Arapaho, Tallahasutci, and Op-
othleyahola, the great Creek leader. Having lived and worked in
the Indian Territory, he spoke bits and pieces of several tribal
languages. He missed talking to his old friends, some of whom
spoke little English, and he feared he was losing what little he
knew of their words through disuse. "The first good crop, we'll
go back to a powwow."

Often a lesson required the whole evening because so many
things reminded Papa of incidents he enjoyed telling.

"T-e-l-e-p-h-o-n-e," I spelled.

"That reminds me of the day Lucy came into the bakery mad-
der than a wet hen," Papa laughed. "She came right in the back.
I'll never forget it. I was just taking some bread out of the oven
and backed up with the peel pole in my hands and bumped her.
She pointed to the telephone on the wall—we had the first one
in town—and said, 'Walt, phone up my lawyer in Ponca City.'
I did. She yelled into the telephone, 'Mr. Gilbert, that you? Black

Wing hit me. Me buy divorce! No. No. No talk. You buy me divorce. I pay.' She hung up the receiver.

"I said, 'Lucy, you and Black Wing are too old to get a divorce. Where'd he hit you?' 'Here. On my arm. Act like white man.' I said, 'Why don't you act like Indian woman and throw his stuff out the door?' 'No,' she said, 'he act like white man. I act like white woman. I buy divorce. No hits, Walt. Black Wing not treat me bad.' I asked her to sit down, and I talked to her a long time, in Oto, mostly about what a good man Black Wing was and what a good woman she was. She was, too. She didn't say anything. When she got up to leave, she looked right at me and said, 'Me buy divorce.' A few days later they came in together to buy some bread and pies and I saw that everything was all right. She went in back and asked your mother to have me call her lawyer and ask him to take the divorce back, that she didn't want it. 'He can give it to someone else,' she said to your mother, 'Black Wing not hit me again—ever.' "

So much for *telephone* and other illustrated words; I could never forget them.

Arithmetic was dramatic. The problems Grandfather gave me were about acres, horses, cows, chickens, prairie dogs, coyotes, skunks, cane, feterita, and broomcorn, which he raised.

"If a rancher had 9,000 acres of grazing land, and an electric storm came up and lightning struck the ground and started a prairie fire, burning 587 acres, how many acres of good grass were left for the stock?"

My imagination was also afire. I visualized the rancher, his family and cowhands, the great roaring windy fires such as I was to see later; I was concerned with the safety of the cattle, with larks nesting in the grass; and there was certain to be a prairie dog town burned over or in danger. The small burrowing owls lived in abandoned prairie dog holes. I had seen them on the mounds surveying their world. Snakes fled to their holes and grasshoppers flew away in a cloud. All creatures that lived in the grass or the earth were fleeing for their lives, and some did not escape. My throat ached with grief. The brave little flowers of the dry plains were killed, but they would come up again in some other spring. Finally, the numbers were seen in a pattern of grass: 8,413 acres gray-green, 587 charred black. The storm was over, and perhaps rain fell, but that was unlikely. Thunder rumbled far off, the great forked bolts of lightning had ceased to split the air, and now only sheet lightning shimmered on the horizon.

"Something more cheerful, now," Grandfather said, and gave me a problem about snowbirds.

When we blew out the lamplight and went to bed, firelight from the stove flickered on the walls. If he were not too tired, he amused Marcy and me by making lifelike shadows with his hands of animal heads. He was very good at it, and we often played this game of shadows until the fire died. There was a loveliness about those evenings when we were all friendly, when the darkness concealed the restraints of the day, when we pushed back the loneliness in the only ways we knew. Now and then, Grandfather sang in a low voice as if to himself, old, sad songs, he said, "from across the sea." Mama sang day or evening; it was her company and her pleasure and her gift. Papa carried in his memory whole narrative poems, poems he had read or listened to around campfires. If the mood was upon him, he suddenly spoke into the darkness, and we, with our heavy comforters pulled up to our chins, as the fire died and the room grew wintry cold, listened, spellbound by the rhythm and the words and the tale, and by his voice so alive that we could believe we saw it all in the dark.

12

On a cold, clear Saturday morning the men placed dry fodder in the wagon bed and Mama spread a comforter over it, while I stood by with another. It was so heavy I could hardly hold it. Mama had made the comforters of wool scraps saved and brought with us from Oklahoma. They were winter quilts, of small patches, in dark colors, blues and browns and black, each patch joined and cross-stitched with red yarn, each patch with a small tie of red yarn in its center. The undersides were plain wool and the insides were made of layers of cotton and wool bought at Tullery's with money from her mother. They were not as pretty as the pieced gay cotton quilts of summer that older women still made on frames at quilting bees, but they were warm and so heavy they must have required a good deal of our energy merely to sleep under them.

In such a country of long winters and brief summers, some said we should have used and worn animal furs. The big wolves had not yet been destroyed or driven to withdraw to the unseen moun-

tains. When repeatedly attacked they left, but the highly intelligent and more cunning coyote stayed in an attempt to outwit
his human enemies. Both wolves and coyotes were numerous
then; they howled in the full-moon nights and they howled in
the howling wind. But it did not occur to us to kill animals as
early trappers had done, and in our hearts we were glad. More-
over, we were the new pioneers, and when we had the money,
we ordered our coats from the mail-order catalogs.

The men were wearing leather caps with fur earmuffs, but none
of our coats save Grandfather's long black greatcoat was warm
enough for the climate. We all wore heavy wool gloves that
Mama and I had crocheted from gray yarn sent us by her mother.
Learning to crochet had made me feel important, in spite of the
fact that the gloves I had made were dotted with many mistakes.
To warm Grandfather's cracked and reddened hands had been my
first incentive, and the gloves he wore were the most knotty and
uneven of all. He did not mind; he praised my efforts and wore
the gloves. Papa and Marcy were very particular about details;
their gloves were perfectly made by Mama. Marcy was the only
spot of color among us; her little coat with brass buttons and her
hood were bright red.

The warm breath of the horses, the dog, ourselves sent misty
clouds into the cold air. The horses jerked their heads and pranced
sidewise, eager for exercise, and Bounce ran about excited to be
going someplace.

"I declare," Grandfather said as we were all ready, "it is too
cold for you womenfolk to go. You may catch your death."

"No worse than dying of lonesomeness," Mama said. "I want
to see if there are still any other people in Colorado." She hoisted
Marcy into the back of the wagon and she and I climbed in. Papa
set the endgate. He went to the front, stepped on the wheel hub,
and leaped up into the spring seat. Grandfather had got up first
and unwound the reins, hopeful of driving his own team.

"We've been to town this fall and winter more than all the
times since I filed my claim. In all these years I was seldom lonesome," he said to Mama. "You'll get used to it."

"I hope not," Mama said.

"Dad has hermit blood," Papa said. "Now, I wasn't built that
way. I have to see some people. But I'll tell you one thing, when
spring comes and I get some chickens, I won't be so lonesome."

Mama made a wry face for me to see.

"There's nothing like chickens to keep you from getting lonesome," Papa said.

Mama covered her mouth, but her laughter burst out, and her lovely eyes were mischievous as I had not seen them for a long time.

"Get up," Grandfather called to the horses, and we were moving toward the gate, toward what was the big adventure of going to town.

"You give them names," Papa went on, "and they like that; they appreciate being called by their own names. Chickens are each one different just like other birds or animals, or people, for that matter."

"Here we go," said Grandfather, making a two-edged remark.

Papa did not care. "People," he said, and it sounded like contumely, "think chickens aren't intelligent, but they are. Not like a dog or a horse or a coyote, but they're not stupid."

The cold ground crackled under the metal rims of the wagon wheels. The snow had melted and blown into small drifts over the gray and somber plain. In back, we tied our scarves high over our faces and settled ourselves wrapped in the quilt. Bounce darted about sniffing game. When he tired, he subsided to a trot behind the wagon. All the sounds of harness and grass and earth were brittle with the long cold. Even the sky seemed brittle, but into its grayness the winter sun was rising. The long morning shadow of the team and wagon and ourselves glided over the buffalo grass beside the road.

Halfway, beyond a low roll of prairie, we passed the prosperous Krouse farm, which could not be seen from our place. None of the few farms on that great plain were in sight of us, giving our world its uninhabited look. Grandfather made a motion at Bounce, and the dog stayed close to the wagon.

"I don't want you chasing any of their stock, you hear?" Without turning to face Mama, Grandfather said, "There are several nice young daughters about your age in that family. Sons all married and gone. I hear one of the girls plays the piano."

Mama rose on her knees and looked at the farm. "Why didn't we come this way before?"

"We're taking the cutoff this morning."

"Don't get your hopes up, Ginny," Papa said. "From what I heard, they might not like their daughters being friends with people who live in a one-room dugout."

"Goddang my wildcats!" Grandfather said.

"Our dugout is clean," Mama said stubbornly. "And we are all decent."

"They have a reputation for being stingy, afraid visitors might want something," Papa said.

"Well, we won't want anything, that's certain, but some company," Mama said and kept looking at the farm with its austere house, large barn, stock pens, and windmill. Near the windmill was a cement milk house. Irrigation ditches ran to a kitchen garden, harvested and dry. Larger ditches, empty and frozen, ran through the alfalfa field that bordered the road.

"Why can't we have that?" I asked.

"We can't buy water."

"*Buy* water?" I was astounded. My impression of water was that it all fell from the sky and ran in streams and rivers. I said as much.

"It does," Papa said. "It's in the ground, too. But this is a dry country, no rain, or only a little. The Krouses buy water from a new dam a long way off. They can afford it. We can't."

That settled it, and I knew better than to ask more questions. By this time, I realized a good deal about the meaning of not being able to afford. What puzzled me was why others might not wish to be friends with us. I ventured to ask that.

"Wellsir," Papa said, "some water running in irrigation ditches in their fields doesn't make them any better than we are. Remember that. But it makes a lot of difference."

If I had been puzzled before, I was a hundred times more puzzled by that judgment, and I was dying to have it explained. But just as I began to speak, Grandfather turned and gave me a look that meant we were together and that I might ask him later.

Mama said, "I suppose when I get acquainted with a few hens and roosters, I really won't mind."

Grandfather chuckled to himself, gazing away from us over the plain as if all that wilderness were his only real friend, the one that understood him and listened. Papa stung Fred and Dip with a flick of the reins.

"None of that, now," Grandfather cautioned.

As we drove even with the house, Mama and I saw a lace curtain drawn back only a little. Someone was watching us pass by.

13

In town, its few people were just beginning their daily work. After the horses were unhitched and tied to the wagon, and hay and water were put down for them, we went our ways, stiff from the cold ride but glad and expectant of the simple pleasure of walking along the two-block main street. As Bounce was not told to stay by the wagon, he bounded away to his own private rambles. Grandfather brought out his small purse and gave Marcy and me each a penny for candy. Our delighted thanks made him smile, and I watched to see his teeth under his black mustache.

"Let's start making our rounds," Papa said, jingling a few silver coins in his pocket. "We'll go see Mrs. Denny and thaw our blood with some hot coffee."

"Best go home early afternoon," Grandfather said. "It'll be quick dark and colder."

Going to Mrs. Denny's Royal Café was like a reunion of old friends. She beamed on us and especially on Mama's simple hood made from her velvet hat.

"Such darlin' extravagance! You ripped up that high-priced city hat and made a common hood, but it'll serve you better here, dear. Only the cowboys wear expensive hats—Stetsons. They put all their money in their hats and boots and saddles. We're just sodbusters." She laughed and her flesh shook.

"Only coffee right now," Papa said. "We'll be back for noon dinner."

"No, you won't, not if you go to Shibley's."

"We like to eat here, Mrs. Denny. We don't take dinner at Shibley's."

"Today you will." Mrs. Denny went to the kitchen, calling back, "You will favor me to taste this gooseberry pie. I'm the only one will eat it."

"I heard that," Papa said.

"You heard nothing of the kind. I just make it for myself and friends. It don't sell. I am making some hot Postum for the little ones. Coffee isn't good for them, you may be too young to know."

"They're as tough as jackrabbits now," Papa said.

Mrs. Denny came back with the pie and Postum, and already it seemed our adventures had begun.

"They look peak-ed to me." She placed her hand on Mama's arm. "I'll bet you don't know how to be poor like plains-poor, you pretty little thing. Now, lay in a supply of cornmeal and a hundred pounds of dried pinto beans, the poor man's meat. It's going to be a long hard winter."

Mama nodded.

"How do you know?" Papa asked.

"I know. I feel it in my bones. And that isn't all. Alonzo, you go over to Doc Burtis. He has some lemons for you. Patient received a crateful from relatives someplace and gave them to Doc to pay for a bill. Doc saved some for you."

Grandfather drank his coffee and rose at once. "I'll be back here around noon to eat. Thank ye, Mrs. D."

Mrs. Denny crossed her big arms on the counter and leaned in front of us. "You know, he'll be a handsome old cuss when he gets that scurvy off. Looks like a Mexican."

"An Indian," I said.

"So that's why he never says anything. Thinking plenty though."

"Black Irish and Welsh," Papa said. "She's got Indians on the brain."

I felt angry but I knew I must behave myself.

"Well, it's nothing to be ashamed of," Mrs. Denny said. "Soon as the Indians are all starved out, people will be claiming relation to them. You'll see."

"I'm not ashamed," Papa said. "Just stating a fact. She's been living with the Otos and now she wants to be one."

Mrs. Denny winked at me, and my anger subsided.

As if to reply to Papa's inevitable question, and to change the subject, she said, "Walt, you know, Mr. Denny has been here twice lately, once during that awful blizzard, but, of course, that doesn't trouble *him*. He saved me and the café from burning up. I fell asleep and the stove was getting away too hot. He kept calling my name, but I didn't see him."

"You don't say."

"Next time, he was right in the room clear as you are, and he told me something that was going to happen and it did."

"Is it anything you can tell us?"

"You'll find it out."

Papa accepted that.

"Do you think the general delivery window is open yet?" Mama asked.

We thanked Mrs. Denny for the good pie and said we'd be back later, but, as she had stated, we did not return that day.

Papa told us to go to the post office while he went on his own errands and to meet him at Shibley's in an hour; then we would go to Tullery's for groceries and leave early for home. I mailed Mama's letters while she received a bundle of ones the postmaster had tied with a string.

"Just about give you up," he said. "You're my best customer. Get snowed in?"

They spoke of the storm, and then Mama paid for a book of two-cent stamps with a two-dollar bill found in her mother's letter. When she dropped the change into her handkerchief and tied two secure knots, she put her forefinger to her lips. I understood. Marcy was running her hands along the mailboxes and did not see our exchange.

We walked around town to use up the hour, and when we

got to Shibley's we saw the black mourning crape on the door.
We hesitated, but since we heard voices within the house, we
knocked and a stranger, a neighbor, opened the door and asked
us in. The house was filled with men and women, talking in low
voices. Women kept coming in bringing dishes of food they set
on the table, which had been lengthened with extra leaves. The
fragrance of coffee and food mingled with that of flowers and a
strangely disturbing medicinal odor. Most of the people were unknown to us.

A woman came up to us and said quietly, "Would you like to
see him?"

"Yes," I said, as Mama hesitated.

"He's in here." She opened a door to the right, let us in, and
closed the door after us.

The window shades were drawn and candles burned on two
high stands. The room was otherwise bare save for a large vase of
wilting hothouse flowers, two chairs, and the black casket. I did
not know to what I had said yes. I had come to see Fred. Marcy
and I spoke often of our make-believe travels in Fred's old wheelchair. Mama went to the casket and drew back, saying, "Oh,
oh—" She took our hands to leave the room but we resisted. I
climbed on a chair and looked in, and there among the crinkled
satin was Fred, so alien and still, his face and hands gray-blue-
white and the texture of cold wax. All the flesh, now unlike flesh,
sank in dark hollows, the temples, the eyes, the cheeks. He was
formal, too, unlike Fred, in his white shirt, black suit, and black
tie. I stared at his still hands until they appeared to move ever so
little. Frightened, I stared at his face again; and then I saw that
one eyelid was not tightly closed and there was his dead eye. It was
so terrible to see that dead eye that the knowledge struck me from
a deep and unknown place that Fred was *dead*. I began to cry. It
seemed to me there was something I should do to bring him back,
but the image of that narrow slit of eye beyond all light and move-
ment, still, still and dead, lodged in my memory and would not
get out. I heard him say, as he had said at the end of every visit,
"Come back again. I'm always home, unless, that is, I am in
Makassar."

Marcy began to whimper. "Is Fred dead the way our cat was
dead that time?" She was afraid.

"He has gone to Makassar, the way he said, remember?" I knew he was dead, but Makassar sounded like a foreign heaven, and Fred was always traveling to strange places.

"Sh-h-h-h," Mama whispered.

When we went out again, among the people who were talking and eating from plates of food forcefully handed them by the women, one asked us kindly to sit down and eat. We could not; our hunger had disappeared. She showed us to the room where Mr. and Mrs. Shibley were, and there, too, was Papa. They had been crying. I did not know that men cried and I could not keep from staring at them.

After Mama had spoken her sympathy, Mrs. Shibley said, and she had a hard time saying it, "Fred and Walter had become such friends even before you girls came, that, that—"

Mr. Shibley was holding her hand and he finished for her. "Walter is going to sit up with Fred tonight."

"You can stay here or with one of the neighbors," Mrs. Shibley said, getting control of her voice.

The other bedroom was Fred's, already made fresh for someone else, but *Fred* was still there. We were dismayed.

Papa said, "Thanks, Mrs. Shibley. But they'd better go on home with Dad." He came into the hall with us. "I'll walk back tomorrow or the next day. If it snows, I'll wait it out." He touched Marcy's upturned, worshipful face. "It won't snow," he told her.

As he turned back to the Shibleys, a woman came with a tray of food. "You must eat something, all three of you, even a little. You'll feel better." She left the tray in their room.

"Who is going to sit up with the dead tonight?" a man asked another.

The cow bawled.

"Oh, that poor Caroline, you'd think she knows."

"She knows," a man said flatly. "Animals know such things."

"Walter Babb and Ernest Dillet," another man answered the first. "I'll tend the cow till the folks take hold."

We were glad to reach the door and step into the cold fresh air. Caroline bawled again. I hoped someone would bring her a cardboard box to eat.

"I'm hungry," Marcy said and began to cry.

"We'll get some cheese and crackers at Tullery's. You can sit by the stove and eat."

Bounce suddenly ran up beside us, joyously alive. He had been wandering the town and was now on his way to the wagon. I hugged him sadly. He was alive. We were all alive. Fred had been alive and now he was dead. I tried to think about it, but it evaded me even as it overwhelmed me with its impenetrable meaning. I could not grasp anything about it but the sorrowful knowledge that Fred was like the rigid meadowlark we found on the range one day, all his magic singing gone. Gone where? The wind was blowing his feathers backward. They riffled as if alive on his still wings, and it was this suggestion of life on that unresponding body that hurt me, that revealed to me for an instant the nature and certainty of death. The meadowlark helped me to understand that *he*, that wintry, unlaughing man, would not renew in the spring as the dry grass under our feet would grow green or the sleeping trees at the creek leaf out again summer after summer after summer.

That still, dead eye had already profaned my memories.

14

WINTER WAS LONG, with cold winds and blizzards and brilliant quiet days. In the land of the big sky, the land is big under it. When earth and sky are locked in cold, the far horizon is lost. We were overwhelmed by distance and circled by chill infinity. The grass, for this was grassland, was gray-brown or white with snow. The wind moved in long aggrieved wails across the plain. Packs of wolves howled. We remembered Old Loony in his shack on the open range and we wondered if he were dead or alive. On our trips between dugout and barn, frost formed on our eyelashes and nostrils and mouth, and we tried to hold our breath against the pure fierce air. The hated dugout became a safe burrow as welcome as that belonging to any animal pursued by the elements. Into this savage season spring burst like a bud. Bright little wild flowers nodded in the tawny grass, prickly-pear cactus put on its waxy yellow bloom, meadowlarks sang from the ground, and chicken hawks and prairie falcons wheeled in the blue sky alert to spring's vulnerable young as they were hatched or born.

White starflowers bloomed at dusk. In its nest of bayonet leaves, a spike of creamy yucca flowers gleamed like a ghostly candle in the early dark.

We listened to the high, concerted honking of Canadian geese migrating home again and watched their arrow formations pierce the sky. As the earth warmed, snakes shed their skins. We found their soft eggs under weeds. Lizards darted in the sun, and a large tortoise crossed our yard on his instinctive way to somewhere. Bounce chased rabbits and went on long rambles in search of mating. Banter's bull was on the range with the herd far to the south. Russian thistles sprang up everywhere, their two dark-green, needle leaves tender and edible. In summer they would become huge tumbleweeds and in autumn they would roll with the wind alone or in flocks across the land. We pulled them up, those two-inch plants, needing thousands to make a meal. Soon they would be too prickly to eat.

The wind became stronger; there was always the wind. The snows had been good, and Papa and Grandfather prepared to plow and plant the fields to broomcorn. Although in dryland farming part of the fields lay fallow each year to catch and store rare moisture, we used a few of those acres to raise feed for the horses: maize, feterita, cane fodder, and corn. We ourselves could hardly wait to eat fresh corn and chew the sweet cane stalks, from which Mama would make syrup for our winter hardtack. The small granary attached to the north side of the barn for a wind-break was nearly empty of fodder and grain. I especially liked to look at the fat white-grained heads of African feterita on their crooked stems.

Grandfather owned a sod-breaker, a lister, and a binder. Breaking sod was very hard work. Papa walked behind the single plow gripping the handles hard, as the slightest neglect permitted the share to leap from the tough virgin soil. The wide flat blade of the sod-breaker cut rectangles of root-matted earth and laid them upside down. There is no furrow in broken sod; the labor of future springs would crumble the slabs of turf, leaving the soil vulnerable in drouth years to hard-blowing winds.

After breaking the sod and broadcasting seed, Papa hitched the horses to the lister to plow the other fields. Marcy and I had been interested in this machine from the first: It had two high wheels and a metal seat, a graceful flared share that plowed a deep fur-

row, a can filled with broomcorn seeds. The seeds dribbled into
the furrow and two small wheels in back controlled an instru-
ment that covered the seeds. We followed the lister; its simul-
taneous activities were like magic. The ground was rich in worms;
no sooner were they exposed than they wriggled back into their
dark home. The fragrance of newly turned earth came back to us.
Our bare feet luxuriated in its soft coolness.

The plow upturned a nest of field mice and we cried out. Papa
called the horses to stop and they stood patiently, glad for the
rest. He got down from the seat and came behind the lister to
see the mice. They were not more than an inch long, huddled
together in a snug nest of sticks and bits of plant down. Two of
them were thrown out of the nest by the giant eruption of their
landscape.

"Poor little things," Papa said, and picked them up gently to
place them with the others. "They'll grow up and eat some of
the grain, but they have a right to live too. Maybe they're good
for something."

Marcy walked up a furrow to get away from the mice and
stepped under Dip, her tow head pressed against the horse's huge
belly. "You kill rattlesnakes," she called.

"I know it," Papa said and would not explain. "Get out from
under that horse so I can get back to work."

She obeyed and move off unhappily toward the dugout, her
hero caught in a contradiction.

"Go with her," Papa told me, "and watch out for snakes. Bring
me back a jug of water." He climbed onto the seat, angry with
himself. "Damn kids. Cheyenne, explain to her about killing rattlesnakes." I thought I might or I might not. Did I really understand why one thing was killed and not another? All ran when
threatened. All wanted to live. At the ends of the field the horses,
all on their own, turned around exactly in place for the next furrow. If I hurried back with the gunny-wrapped jug, I would be
in time to watch them at the next turn. "Go on," Papa said.
"You've got to look after her; she's just a little sprout."

When we were partway across the field, we saw a cowboy riding from the direction of Two Buttes and were amazed to see
him open our gate and ride in. Mama came up from the dugout
to greet him. The cowboy took off his big hat in a courteous gesture and handed Mama something we couldn't see. He was al-

ready riding south when we reached the yard, where Mama was still standing.

"He brought me a note from the Krouse girls, from Maxine; they want us to come for a visit some afternoon." She was smiling. "Would you like to go?"

"No," Marcy said.

"Yes," I said.

Marcy went into the dugout.

"Well, what's the matter with her?"

"It's something about mice and snakes." I wanted to hear Papa tell it.

"I see, said the blind man." Mama sort of danced down the steps, singing in her high soprano, "Oh, la, la, la, la, la, la!"

I filled the jug at the water barrel and poured a dipper of water over the gunnysack wrapped and sewed in place around it to keep its contents cool. Then I walked along the fence where the ground was hard and it was easier to carry the jug. I was nearly even with Papa's furrow when I saw a speck on the road to the north. The speck soon became Old Loony with a pack of supplies on his back. No better luck could I have had that day than to be able to see Old Loony again just across the fence, very close, and yet be safe from his mysterious craziness because Papa was there. Papa was still halfway down the field, but the team was approaching steadily. I lay down on a newly plowed ridge and waited, enjoying the good smell of earth, the feel of it along my back and bare legs, and the sight of the blue spring sky with its great white thunderheads.

Papa and Old Loony arrived almost at the same time. Papa drank from the jug and kept the cork out until Loony came even with us.

"Good day, sir," Papa said. He always said "sir" to anyone older than he.

Loony looked at us suspiciously and barely nodded.

Papa went to the fence and held out the jug. "You must need a drink of water walking clear from town. Set your supplies down and rest awhile."

Loony kept going his silent way. Papa set the jug down by a fence post. In his friendly nature there was no room for rebuffing another man as he had been rebuffed by Old Loony. He looked at me and said, "Well, you see how it is." I knew I was expected to understand this characteristic remark, as perplexing to me as Loony's silence. Papa laughed just a little. "Well, at least he isn't dead."

"He is crazy," I said.

"Well, so am I, or I wouldn't be here." Papa looked up at the sky and all around over the fresh brown field. "In the spring here, you could swear this is God's country." He patted the resting horses and they roused themselves for work. I went along with them, sometimes at the side, sometimes following. I was filled with a sense of being and perhaps Papa was too. We were not separate from all of nature; we were not looking on, we were a part.

15

"You'll have to eat more now, Ginny," Papa said. We were having our midday meal of coarse greens from the creek.

"If I remember rightly," Grandfather said, "you should be drinking milk. Some say yes, and some say no." He was careful not to rile Papa.

"Well, these leaves will make some good milk, as grass makes it in cows. Did you ever think of that, Ginny?"

Mama said nothing.

"We can't raise vegetables without water," Papa said. "But you've got to eat better all summer. We're going to have a crop, so we can buy a little more from Tullery."

"A woman needs to get out once in awhile," Grandfather dared. "You can combine the visit with buying a gallon of milk." He opened his small purse, took from its few coins a dime, and laid this beside Mama's plate. "That is the market price."

"It will be a boy," Papa said, and his face was alight and smiling. "He'll be a baseball player. I'll train him. I'll make a big-leaguer out of him. I can do it. I always wanted a boy."

Marcy hit him hard on the arm. Papa hardly noticed. She hit him again.

"This boy—we'll call him Rex—will make you two girls take a back seat. I don't want you mothering him, understand? You can play with dolls. I don't want any sissy."

"I don't like dolls," I said. "I like Pinto Boy."

"Well, that pony is a thing of the past."

"When is Rex coming?" Marcy asked. Her eyes were shiny but she hid the tears by butting her head against Papa.

Papa put his arm around her. "Later this summer. Your mother is showing. Don't you see?"

"Well, now—" Grandfather began.

Papa laughed. "Marcy, your mother has a pumpkin under her apron, but this one will be ripe long before Halloween."

"Well, for heaven's sake," Mama said, getting up from the table. I looked for the hidden pumpkin. "Baseball players, a Halloween pumpkin, what next? Has it occurred to you, Walt, what it means to have a new baby in this hole in the ground?" She touched Grandfather's shoulder. "I'm sorry."

Papa's face was blank with surprise. "Why, he'll be a lot of fun."

"You didn't say that the two times before, and we weren't poor at all, then."

"Well, this one will be a *boy*."

"It still takes a woman to have one, and I wish I could have a whole litter of nine, and you could have your precious ball team!"

Papa looked at Grandfather and smiled. "She's got her dander up. Looks like she did when I met her. You see, it does her good."

"Great Scott!" Mama said and went up the steps, saying in a low voice, "This poor baby doesn't know what he's getting into."

Papa wrote in his small notebook for the first time since the death of Fred Shibley. This time his face was lighted by thoughts of posterity.

The three of us wore freshly ironed dresses and sunbonnets, and Mama had polished her shoes. Marcy and I walked in clean bare feet on the dry road. I carried a shiny gallon pail for milk, and

Mama pulled a long-handled child's cart for Marcy, who was too young to walk all the way. The early-summer day was clear and pleasantly warm and oddly without wind. That made walking easy.

"Our little trip has turned out to be a lark," Mama said.

To pass our field and see the good stand of broomcorn started us off in glad spirits. Beyond our fence the road lay on the open range and all along its edges we saw the busy life in the grass. Large red ants far from their tunneled hills hurried about with such apparent purpose they made us laugh. They had not a moment to spare. Some labored with the weight of sticks or prey. Others fought. Their painful sting prompted us to step cautiously when we encountered such an army on the march. Farther along a beetle intently rolled his pellet of dung. Scaled bugs that looked like fishes followed one another in a line. Lizards flashed by, then stopped, waiting with lifted heads to watch us pass.

When we came to the fenced, irrigated alfalfa fields, dark green and fragrant, four miles were behind us, and the big house was near. A white-rumped shrike was busily catching grasshoppers and impaling them on the barbs of the fence.

One of the Krouse girls, Maxine, came out to meet us, and it was clear that she was glad for company. Mama mentioned the cowboy who had brought her note, and the girl raised a finger to her lips and blushed. Mama nodded. Maxine led us through a back screened porch into a large room adjoining the kitchen. Fresh-baked bread cooled on a long table under sunny windows and its fragrance roused our hunger. Cleanliness was on the room like a carved pattern.

"You must be tired; sit here and rest. I'll be right back. Do you girls want to come along?" We went with Maxine to the milk house near the windmill, into its dusky cold. Water ran through a long cement trough in which were crocks of milk and butter and other perishable food. A crock of eggs gleamed in the corner. Marcy and I were fascinated with the running water. Maxine carried a large white pitcher into the house and poured cool buttermilk into six glasses and sliced the soft warm bread onto flowered plates. She spread butter thickly and carelessly.

"Maxine!"

"Yes, Mama." She seemed to know what was wanted without further words.

The tall, large-boned woman stood in the doorway between this sunny room and the kitchen and nodded to Mama, saying, "I'm pleased to meet you, Mrs. Babb." Mama rose and walked over to her with her greeting. Mrs. Krouse looked at Marcy and me with approval. We were clean and we sat on her clean chairs in polite silence.

When Maxine handed her mother a glass of buttermilk, the woman said, "I don't need it. Now, excuse me." She returned to the kitchen. Another daughter, Pearl, came in at that moment and greeted us in a friendly way. She and Maxine placed the glasses and plates on a large round table covered with blue oil-cloth, and we began to eat the thick slices of bread so generously buttered. Maxine brought the white pitcher to the table, filling all the glasses as soon as they were empty. She buttered more bread for Marcy and me. We were brimming with pleasure, shy to express it, but that did not matter. The two girls and Mama were talking and laughing, and Mama sounded like a young girl, too.

"We could go in the parlor," Pearl said after a bit.

We followed her into a dark, dank room with heavy furniture and drawn blinds, and a flowered carpet under our feet. Family pictures in thick wooden frames hung on the walls. A piano loomed from a corner.

"We can't have any fun in here," Maxine said. "I hate all this gloom. Pearl, we ought to have the piano moved up to our sitting room, then we could play and sing in the light of day."

Mama was looking at the piano.

"Next time you come," Maxine said, "we'll play and sing. But today, let's talk and get acquainted."

We left the dark room and climbed an enclosed staircase that led to a narrow hall at one end of which was a large sunny room. Closed doors indicated other bedrooms. After the dugout, this much space was almost unbelievable.

"Are they secret rooms?" Marcy whispered to me, walking close to the wall opposite the closed doors.

"No. Why are you always afraid, silly?"

"Because."

She wanted me to say, "Because why?" but this house was far too interesting for us to start playing a game and perhaps miss seeing something. It was large like Grandma Greenberry's house but not as pretty.

"This was Mama's sitting room but she never used it, so now

we girls have it for our very own. Mama says it is a waste of time to sit down in the daylight."

"Maxine," Pearl scolded her sister. "Our mother is happiest working."

Two beds were covered with bright crazy quilts, hand-sewn by the girls, as Pearl explained. The wide floorboards were scrubbed of all color; crocheted rugs shone like valentines. Two flowery little rockers with sewing baskets beside them rested primly in the sun. Hemstitched yellow curtains hung at the windows.

"Sit there, if you like, girls," Pearl told us, pointing to two footstools. We faced the windows in order to feel the excitement of looking down upon the landscape. This was quite different from looking along the ground from our dugout window into the world of ants and tarantulas and snakes.

Mama and Pearl sat in the rockers, and Pearl reached into her basket and took out a shuttle and began tatting lace. The lace she had made was rolled up and pinned, already long and of very fine white thread. I turned away from the window to watch her hand send the shuttle flying forward and back, forward and back, the new lace growing before my eyes; and I vowed to learn to tat as soon as we could afford to buy a shuttle and thread. I did not care about the lace so much as I cared about making it; I would give it to Mama.

Mama surprised me by bringing from her pocket a crochet needle and white yarn. She was making a small boot.

"Umm-huh," Pearl said. "Won't be long."

Maxine sat down on a large wooden chest, one of the two in the room. "What shall we talk about?"

"I suppose you would like to talk about Cooper Loveland. You're sitting on your hope chest," Pearl said drily.

Maxine giggled and kicked her heels softly against the wood. "Cooper brought you the note."

"Oh," Mama said. "He's a manly-looking boy."

"See!" Maxine laughed and lay back on the hope chest and kicked her feet into the air.

"Behave yourself! You are the limit. What will Mrs. Babb think? Sit up!"

Maxine was blushing and she seemed to be laughing all over. Mama smiled at her.

"Some say he has Indian and maybe Mexican blood," Pearl said. "A little, anyway."

"What of it?" Maxine sat up. "Aren't we all alike?"

"True, sister, but that doesn't cut a bit of ice with Papa and Mama. Besides, he has no land. Anyone we marry, Mrs. Babb, must have some land. Papa won't hear of it otherwise."

"He'll have land. Land. Land. Land."

"He's a working cowboy."

"Work is honorable," Mama said.

The girls looked at Mama with respect, as much for her comment as for her position as a married woman.

"I have heard that most cowboys dream of owning their own ranches," Mama said. "Is that the way with Cooper Loveland?"

"He doesn't even know I exist," Maxine said gaily.

"It's just a matter of time, the way you looked at him last Fourth of July in town, and when you stopped him to deliver our note."

"I was proper."

"Just barely."

"I am ready to go to the wedding," Mama joked.

Maxine got up and looked out the window. "Imagine!"

"She has it bad," Pearl said, going to Maxine's hope chest and raising the lid.

Maxine came running. "Don't you dare!" They pulled and pushed each other, laughing, and Pearl won. She lifted the lid and snatched a small square of linen, tossing it over Maxine to Mama. It was heavily embroidered and in the center was an embroidered name: Mrs. Cooper Loveland.

"Don't ever, ever tell, *please*, Mrs. Babb. That would make him hate me."

"I won't, don't worry yourself. I wish you girls would call me Ginny."

"Our hope chests are stuffed full of linens we've made and embroidered for our future homes, and I used to say, when they got to the top, it will happen. We'll just naturally be engaged or married."

"You both will," Mama said. "You're young."

"I am older than Maxine but I am not ready yet. I want to stay with Mama and Papa as long as I can."

"And Pearl should marry first, being older. That's what Mama and Papa believe."

"They won't mind when the time comes," Mama said.

"Well, for me the time has come, and I want Cooper Loveland, I don't care a hang if that sounds bold or not. Do you think I am bad"—she hesitated—"Ginny?"

"Of course not!"

Maxine sighed. "I envy you." She looked straight at Mama's rounded belly.

"Now, Maxine! That will be quite enough. That is no way for a single girl to talk, for heaven's sake." Pearl's face and neck were red. "I wonder what you think of us? We heard you come from a very proper family."

"They are very nice; seven of us, and we were happy together. You girls remind me of my sister and me and our friends."

"Do we, really?"

"You must enjoy yourselves all you can while you are young. Life is serious soon enough and it can be very hard sometimes. I remember when I was in love."

"You mean it won't last at all?" Maxine blurted out. "That's what Pearl keeps telling me."

"Being in love is the first part, but it lasts in another way, other ways as the years go by, and it's all love. Unless it goes bad."

"You look like a girl," Maxine said, "and you know all that about love."

"Not very much, really. But I was married when I was fifteen. I was as crazy about Walt as you are about Cooper, and in the ten years since, I guess I've loved him in a dozen different ways."

"What does that mean?" Maxine asked eagerly.

"Oh, sometimes more, sometimes less, and sometimes not at all, and then in different ways I don't know how to explain, but the main thing is I love him."

"You see!" Maxine looked at her sister.

"There are some married people who don't love each other, of course," Mama said.

"*Are there?*" Maxine spoke each word with emphasis, and her eyes opened so round that Mama and Pearl laughed.

Maxine picked up her embroidered square and held it against her breast. "I put this under my pillow every night. It's like sending him a message."

"Maybe he is afraid to call on you or ask you out," Mama said.

"Cooper Loveland afraid! Why on earth?"

"Because your folks have so much, and he has just his horse and saddle."

"He has his self-respect!"

"Girls! Girls!" Their mother was calling from the foot of the stairs.

Maxine quickly replaced her treasure in the hope chest, and we all hurried downstairs.

"Time is going by," Mrs. Krouse said. "Did you young ladies have a good visit?"

We all answered yes at once.

"Well, that's nice, but you forgot the time. It is nearly supper-time, and Mrs. Babb will have to be getting home."

"Is it that late? I'm sorry."

"It doesn't matter," Pearl said, trying to cover her mother's suggestion.

"It is clouding up," Mrs. Krouse continued, "and they'll want to be going before supper."

"We didn't come for supper," Mama said calmly, but her sensitive face showed hurt. "I do want to buy a gallon of milk if you can spare it."

Maxine grabbed the pail from the table and ran to the milk house; she was back in a few minutes. "From us to you," she said.

A deep roll of thunder sounded. The sunlight that was bright in the room and over the long table of bread dimmed to a blue shadow.

"You mustn't go!" Maxine said.

"It is nearly suppertime." Mrs. Krouse's words were so placid that the next roll of thunder startled us all. "It is far-off yet," she said.

Mama gave her the dime. Mrs. Krouse held it a moment, then dropped the coin into her apron pocket.

"Thank you all for a lovely visit." Mama's smile was full and sincere.

The mother nodded and turned back into the kitchen. We went outside and Mama settled Marcy into the cart. I was to carry the milk. The girls asked Mama to come again soon. They looked at the sky. It was still light above us, but dark clouds gathered in the distance and lightning shimmered. The sun came out again.

"We'll get home all right." Mama started for the gate.

"I'll go with you." Maxine ran after us.

"Maxine!" her mother called. Pearl waved us an anxious goodbye but Maxine came with us onto the road.

"Go back now," Mama told her. "Mind, you don't forget Cooper Loveland."

They laughed and Maxine ran back to the house, turning and waving and calling.

16

"THAT IS THE LAST TIME we will go there," Mama said to me. "And I like those girls. Now, let's walk as fast as we can to get away from this fence and the telephone wires."

Horses in the pasture were running around crazily, kicking up their heels, the way they do before a storm. The cattle on the range to the right of us were restless; young steers were running and switching their tails hard.

Weeds beside the road trembled in a small wind and then the air was still again, too still. We had reached the open plain when the first large drops of rain fell and suddenly stopped. A sharp clap of thunder filled the sky and dark clouds traveling fast covered the sun. In this stormy shade a brilliant clarity spread over the plain; everything near and far could be seen in precise detail. We began to run. Marcy clung to the sides of the jolting cart, and from under the loosened lip of my pail milk leaped out and splattered the ground. Forked lightning cracked the sky and heavy

thunder followed. We stopped for an instant to slow our painful
breath, then we ran faster.

The turmoil in the clouds frightened us. They appeared to boil
and grew blacker every moment. We could feel the terrible wind
held back, ready to break upon us. Suddenly the lightning flashed
in great bolts all around us; jagged blades split the black sky and
lighted the plain more brightly than the sun. Thunder roared and
clapped and shook the air. Far ahead we saw the electricity run
along our fence. Then a great flash blinded us. The lightning
speared the ground and stood rooted for an instant. The bolt
and the thunder deafened us. The air smelled of burning. We
were paralyzed by the shock. Then Mama pulled the cart onto
the grass and took Marcy into her arms.

"Put down the pail! It's metal. Leave the cart!"

Marcy was too heavy to be carried but her baby legs could not
run fast enough to keep up with Mama and me, and Mama held
her close and ran. The clouds lowered and blackened. Suddenly
the wind broke over us with such violence that we fell against it,
trying to push our bodies a step farther toward home. At last we
lay on the ground, unable to go on. When we were rested a little,
we rose and tried to walk. The wind pitched us back and thrust
us from side to side but we kept on. Then the clouds opened and
rain fell upon us in wind-driven torrents. We had spoken only
the few necessary words all the way, silenced by fright. Sometimes
the three of us walked holding hands, but that was too slow. Although we were drenched, and bruised, we were comforted a little
by the lessening of the lightning after the rain began.

We heard a sound through the violence of the storm that was
not of the storm. We heard it again, but we could not see through
the downpour. Then we heard a shout far off, a shout and curses,
and the beating of horses' hoofs, the sound of the wagon.

"Oh, thank God!" Mama said and sat down beside the road.

The horses lunged through the rain into view. Papa was urging
them and striking them with the stinging ends of the lines. The
wagon rumbled and shook as if it would fall apart. Papa was
standing up; water ran over his dark hair, soaking it down; he
had forgotten his cap. The worry on his face changed to anger
as he jerked the horses to a stop and looked down upon us.

"Didn't you have sense enough not to start out in this storm?"

He leaped from the wagon and almost threw Marcy and me over the sides and helped Mama into the seat.

"It came up suddenly after we left," was all Mama said.

"I got worried and went out to watch, but I thought you'd see it coming up and stay there till I came after you."

"Papa," Marcy yelled up to him on the high seat, "we left the milk and my cart on the prairie."

"To hell with them! I'll get them when the storm's over." He slashed the lines on the horses' rumps and turned the wagon around so sharply that for a moment it threatened to go over. The horses were lathered but the rain washed away the foam. He forced them into a run, then as the rain slackened, pulled them to a trot. They were eager to get home and went the rest of the way without direction. Papa was still excited but his anger had calmed. "I wouldn't have seen you at all if it hadn't been for the lightning just before the rain. I saw you running. Damn fools. You don't know this country. You should have stayed."

"Mrs. Krouse told us to go," I shouted over the sounds of rain and horses and wagon.

"Nobody would do that," he said.

"She did." I wanted to help Mama, who was too much humiliated to tell him.

"Well, I heard she was sure stingy, but damn it to hell, that's the goddamn limit."

"Calm down," Mama said gently. "That's her way. The girls were very nice."

"Damn poor way."

"Papa," Marcy yelled, "you had better quit swearing so much."

Papa laughed. "Well, you're all safe. I'll quit." He looked at Mama. "Are you all right, Ginny?"

"I'm all right."

Grandfather was waiting for us at the door of the doghouse. He came out and asked us if we were all right, then he unhitched the horses at once and took them to the barn. We changed into dry clothes, and Papa made Mama lie down to rest. He prepared hot tea for her from sage we had gathered and dried. I went to the barn to help Grandfather rub down the horses. The rain had stopped. The wind had died down and clouds were racing away from the sun. The sky was clean and blue, and only at the horizon, far off, sheet lightning winked.

"Rub Fred," Grandfather said as soon as I reached the barn door. "He's all excited." Fred swung his great head around and looked at me with wild eyes. I got on my stool and put my arms around his neck and rubbed his long nose, holding my hand on the soft part and talking to him until he stopped trembling.

17

THAT NIGHT I DREAMED of the storm, and somewhere beneath the crackle of lightning and the loud claps and rolls of thunder was the insistent sound of someone injured. The plain was dark, and even in the charged blue flashes I could not find the one who suffered. Because there was no place to hide on the plain, it seemed to me that the cry was disembodied, especially when it grew and grew and filled the sky. Running was useless, the land stretched flat and far in every direction, and when the lightning stopped, the dark was black and furry. I was desperately alone and stiff with terror. I awoke. The voice was in the room, a low moaning that filled the small dugout. Grandfather was shaking me gently. He was dressed and the lamp was burning. The moaning stopped.

"Get up," he whispered to me, "and find some clean rags." He began to build the fire quickly, with none of his usual ceremony. As soon as the flames caught, he went up the steps with the water bucket.

As I sat on the creaky wire cot trying to understand what was wanted of me, Papa, still in his underwear, dropped Marcy into the quilts behind me. His excitement brought me fully awake.

"Get Marcy under the covers! Cover up her head!" Marcy was half-asleep but she looked frightened. I saw Flossie, her rag doll, somehow fallen into the woodbox. Marcy must have been holding her in her sleep. I handed Flossie to her and Marcy crawled under the quilts. I covered her head.

"Help Flossie go to sleep, Marcy," Mama called. Her voice was tired.

I went over to Mama's bed and she smiled at me and put her hand on my cheek. "Don't be afraid. I'll be all right. You've been sick and you got all right, didn't you?"

I nodded, but I was afraid. I remembered the moaning in my dream. Papa had grabbed his shirt and overalls off a nail on the back of the door and was already dressed.

"Be a big girl, Chey, and help Papa."

Mama's face began to perspire and she wadded a piece of the pillowcase hem and bit it hard. I brought the clean rags. Papa drew back her covers, lifted her, and told me to place newspapers thickly on the blanket and to spread the clean rags on the papers. He lowered her gently and the papers crackled. Our bedclothing, like all the rest of our necessities, being limited, we had to take extra precautions.

Grandfather had water boiling on the stove and a clean wash-pan nearby. I wondered what the steaming water was for, but I asked no questions. The atmosphere in the crowded room was becoming more strained. Mama cried out sharply, then pressed her knuckles against her mouth and moaned, trying not to. Papa rushed to her and commanded, "Don't move, Ginny. Hold him back! Hold him back!"

"Who?" I whispered to Grandfather. He shook his head for me to keep quiet.

"Rex," Papa said, "your brother."

"You may as well know," Grandfather said. His face and voice were sad and disapproving.

"She knows," Papa said, emphasizing both words. "She hid behind a curtain and watched Marcy being born."

Grandfather looked at me.

"It was scary," I told him.

"Served you right," Papa said.

"I wanted to see Rex."

Grandfather clucked his tongue.

"Well, by God, this time it will be Rex."

Mama laughed and her laughter was twisted with pain. "It was terrible and funny too. Chey came out from behind the curtain, pale and big-eyed, and handed a red apple to the doctor for the baby. He nearly had a fit. We all did."

"Be quiet, Ginny. Lay still."

She began to perspire again and Grandfather told me to bathe her face with cool water.

"Goddang my wildcats," he said as if he had made up his mind, "I better drive to town and get Doc Burtis."

"Wait till daylight," Papa said. "Nobody can do anything right now. It's all up to Ginny."

"Well, for the love of pete," Mama said.

"I mean, just don't move and he will be all right."

Grandfather sat down on the cot, took out his pipe, and quickly put it back again. Papa began to play solitaire at the kitchen table.

"Go to bed, Cheyenne," Mama said, and I lay down and fell asleep at once.

When I woke up, the lamp was still burning, the window showed the dark, and the moaning was strong now, filling the room. Papa was busy. An odor of new blood was bitter in the air. I got up quickly, not sure why. No one paid any attention. Mama screamed again and again without apology, without remembering us, alone in her pain. She stopped suddenly.

"It's all over," Papa said after awhile, and his voice shook so much that Grandfather made a rare gesture. He laid his long brown hand on Papa's shoulder for an instant and said, "Son. Son."

That was the most unfortunate word he could have uttered. Papa jerked away from him and sat down on a lard can and covered his face with his hands. It was terrible to hear him sobbing. I tiptoed over to Mama and bathed her face. She was exhausted and could not even cry. Her hair and the pillow were wet with perspiration and her eyes kept closing as if she were falling asleep. The bed was soaked with water and blood; the little baby so nearly completed lay there untended. The scene on the bed was awesome and frightening. Mama struggled to sit up and cover herself. Papa's crying slowed; he wiped his face and blew his nose and set to work. He did not know what to do but with Mama's help he did it. We made the bed as clean and dry as possible and helped Mama into another nightgown.

"Shall I make you a cup of weed tea?" Grandfather asked, trying to cheer her. She nodded yes.

"What'll I wrap him in, poor little naked man. A towel?"

"No, no," Mama said, "use the linen pillowcase I embroidered. Get it, Cheyenne."

Papa washed him. "Look at his fingers!" he said in wonder to himself. He wrapped him in a small towel, then put him in the pillowcase, winding it round and round until the embroidered hem showed. Mama bit her lip and turned her face away.

"Go along to hold him," she said to me.

The night air was sharp with the smells of sage and sun-baked land released by the rain. A last-quarter moon was going down. Stars swung through the curving dark. For all that had happened, I could not ignore the beauty of the night; I was glad to be in it, free of our room. Papa carried the spade and the baby. I followed him south to an open space in the field near the fence, just beyond the green cane. Except for the small cracking sounds I thought of as the cane growing, the night was still.

He handed me the baby and set the spade to the ground, placing his right foot on the rim to push it down. Then he stopped with both hands on the handle, his foot still on the spade, and forgetting we were there, he stared into the sloping dark.

This boy, who would have carried his name, aroused thoughts of his own existence that I found in Papa's notebook later. He had waited for Rex, and Rex's life and death had been all in an instant. It made him aware of every suffering life on earth. He had never felt them personally before. The awesome bigness of all the pain, the cruelty, the sorrow was too much to feel. The only way to endure it was not to add to it, but could he keep to that? Was his life of any other significance in the whole incredible pattern? That was all he had, and he needed to grasp something right now, to help him get back to the size of his own life.

It was hard to let go of his son. Even if they had another son, he would not be this one. Did the very brevity of this child's life have a purpose, and was that purpose to shake his bare soul in this bare night and leave it wondering?

This was his son as he was his father's son. What was Alonzo thinking as he sat for long periods, his eyes filled with distance? Were they, father and son, thinking the same old thoughts of his grandfathers before him and his children ahead? If so, they would never let each other know. Papa didn't know why, but they wouldn't—couldn't. He only knew now that he was something more than he could name, something more than he was yesterday.

The baby was still warm and supple in my arms. At first I had held him gingerly, but without knowing it, I was holding him close against my chilled body.

Papa began to dig a hole. Beneath the thin dampness, the ground was cold and dry and resisted the spade. He threw his strength against it. The hole grew larger than was needed and he gathered some last-year's cane stubble and lined it like an animal's burrow. On his knees, he perfected the bed. The bundle I held was growing heavier and had lost its warmth. Dawn was gray and ugly. I began to shiver. Papa reached out and I placed Rex in his hands. I watched the embroidered shroud of white flowers and leaves disappear beneath a thick layer of cane stalks. Papa drew the dirt into the grave, spreading and pressing it until it was as smooth as the earth around it. He placed a rock there and spoke to me for the first time. "We'll get some rocks at the creek today and make a mound, make it safe from Bounce and coyotes." The sun was coming up and fragrance rose from the earth into the crystal air. Without looking at the sunrise, Papa got up and went to the barn to write in his notebook; to add his thoughts on the loss of his son to those on his expected birth, and to those on the death of Fred Shibley; to his record of drouths and storms, eclipses and warnings, crops and old verses.

When I went back across the field and into the dugout, Grandfather was putting cow chips in the fire. Coffee was perking, its good morning smell covering the odor of blood. Marcy was still under the quilts asleep. Mama was sleeping, her face flushed and blue shadows under her eyes. Her lips were parted and dry. I had never seen her look this way.

"Your mother is sick," Grandfather said. "Put your hand on

her forehead. She has a high fever. I'm going to town shortly to get her some medicine from Doc Burtis. You stay here and look after her. Where's your father?"

"In the barn."

"I'm sorry for him, but it's mighty hard for us to speak a solemn word to each other."

"Why?"

"Father and son. That's as good an answer as any."

18

WHILE GRANDFATHER WAS HITCHING UP the horses that morning, Carrie Mayo Whitehead drove into our gate in her new spring wagon pulled by two beautiful bays.

"Where are you going, Alonzo, when you ought to be in the fields?"

He told her about Mama. She tied the reins and leaped down. "Go on to work. I'll go see Dr. Burtis. Keep an eye on the bays."

"A new rig."

She laughed. "Jim gave them all to me for coming back. I was coming back anyway."

She ran to the dugout and down the steps, and I with her. When she saw Mama, she said, "My land, Ginny! I came by to take you to town with me. I thought we'd have a lark before all the harvest work."

Mama felt too bad to speak but she tried to smile. Carrie put her hand on Mama's forehead. "Good land! You're burning up! Now listen, Ginny, you drift off to sleep and don't worry about anything. I'll get Doc Burtis out here. That man can cure anything. It's seven miles there and seven miles back, so sleep."

She gave me directions and ran up the steps, bumping into Papa on the way down.

"Dad's going into town," he said as if he didn't want to be obligated.

"You men don't know about these things. I'm going. I was already on my way. Get some sleep."

"Don't boss *me* around, Carrie."

"I don't boss Jim. I just won't let him boss me. There's a difference." She smiled and placed a hand on his arm. "Grandad told me what happened, Walt. I'm really sorry. Look after Ginny." She hurried outside, and almost at once I heard the horses trotting toward the road.

Dr. Burtis arrived in a Ford touring car. He came down into the dugout, carrying his black leather bag. Mama had been talking in delirium. "Shibley brought me," Dr. Burtis said. "My buggy was too slow. Babb, your little daughter would like to sit in the car but she won't get in unless you're there. I'll see you on the way out."

Papa left. Dr. Burtis looked at me but I did not leave. "Are you the nurse?" I began to feel frightened of what he would ask of me and of what was in the black bag. "All right, then, I will ask you to help me. A pan of good warm water." He removed his coat and rolled up his white shirt sleeves. I had never seen anyone wash his hands for so long a time. I handed him a clean towel. "Good girl. Scrub the pan. Hotter water. Set it here, while I see after your mother. I've brought everything else I'll need, so you may go sit in the car."

I climbed on the box under the window, keeping my back to him, and looked out along the ground. Usually, watching this busy scene of the bug world was one of our most entertaining pastimes, but now I concentrated on listening to Dr. Burtis. He was a big man who moved with calm efficiency, and he was very busy for awhile. I could hear him breathing. A strong medicinal odor filled the air. Finally, I heard him sit down by the bed and I knew he was looking at Mama. She was quieter, and he began to speak to her in a very gentle way, cajoling and humorous. I looked around and saw her eyes fill with recognition, surprise, relief, and then tears.

"No tears, please: a smile. Listen to me, young lady. I want you to stay in bed until I tell you to get up. No cheating. If we had a hospital, I'd put you in it. You're going to be fine, but I don't need to tell you you're sick, do I? I'm leaving medicine and strict directions with the men and this little nurse here." How ready I was to do his command! He rose and prepared to leave. "I'll be back tomorrow."

"Tomorrow?" Mama spoke for the first time. "That long way?"

"Shibley will bring me again in his car. He is lonesome for Fred and glad to help out."

This extraordinary second call worried Mama. "Will I get my strength back by harvest? I have to!"

"Indeed you will. But right now, we must give nature a chance to burn up and cool down."

"All right."

"That's better. Rest, sleep all you can. It's sleep that knits up the raveled sleeve of care, though I think I've garbled Shakespeare. I'm forgetting."

"Thank you, Dr. Burtis," Mama said weakly, but she was smiling. "And Mr. Shibley, too."

Dr. Burtis made a slight bow, holding his hat in his hand until he reached the outdoors. I followed him up the steps and listened as he spoke to Papa. "She's a very sick girl. I will be back tomorrow. You must . . ." I went back to Mama, my fears renewed, and yet unable to stay awake another minute. Mama was sleeping, perhaps from medicine the doctor had given her. When I woke up, Papa told me that Carrie Mayo Whitehead had stopped by and left, as she put it, "just some neighborly food." Even at my age, I realized that she was being careful of Papa's pride; but we all knew, too, that when the woman of the house is down, neighborly help is right and proper. He could not object.

Mr. Shibley brought Dr. Burtis again the next day, and several times after that, and Mama began to feel well enough to worry about the doctor bill. Papa was so delighted by the growing broomcorn and so grateful that Mama was improving that his gloomy moods over the loss of his son were less frequent and severe.

The summer nights were clear and still and beautiful, and now and then without a word to any of us, Grandfather went for long walks over the plain.

"I wouldn't go away out there at night for anything on earth," Mama said when he was gone, but she said nothing in his presence.

"That's his business if he wants to walk around out there," Papa said. "I kinda like nights myself, but they're lonesome enough right here."

When Grandfather and I were alone, I asked to go along, but he said, "Some other year maybe. I walk too far for you now."

"I can walk far."

"We'll see."

But he did not invite me.

When Mama was up, sitting in the short, hot shade of the dugout, walking more every day, beginning to feel her natural strength again, we had another misfortune that saddened us all and made us, already poor, only poorer. Our horse Fred, my favorite, lay down on the prairie and died. His behavior had given us no warning, or Grandfather would have doctored him or gone to town for the veterinarian. Fred lay just outside the fence, on his way back to the barn, his great white body remindful of the power that had gone out of him with his breath. His eyes that had responded so wildly to excitement were open, and their expression was not one of pain or fright but of gentle acceptance. I sat at his head, stroking his ears that had not yet stiffened, my tears falling and running fast through his white hairs in a small game of hide-and-seek. Grandfather stood looking down at Fred as if he could not yet absorb this staggering event. A great involuntary sigh, almost like one of Fred's own, came from him. He took out his pocketknife and opened the blade.

"You'd best go in now."

"Why?" I protested.

"I'm going to cut the coins out of Fred's shoulder. I don't like to do it."

I left. I could not bear to see the blood or the indignity done to my old friend. Fred had worked hard, I thought, and now his shadow is running about on a green pasture in horse heaven. I tried to think of that instead of the strangely still Fred back there. Dip, alarmed and skittish, had been led to the barn by Papa. Dip drank but would not eat. Bounce, who usually stayed close to Grandfather, cowered away from Fred and came with me to the barn. Dip had broken free of his stall and was standing in the doorway. I spoke to him and tried to get him to back into the barn, but instead he lifted his head and whinnied again and again.

When Grandfather came into the dugout later, after trying to quiet Dip, he washed the coins, which were silver quarters, and handed one to Marcy and one to me for keepsakes. We wrapped them in bits of cloth and placed them in our small empty purses. They were never to be spent but kept in memory of Fred.

"Why did they hurt him?" I wanted to know, hurting with Fred's long-ago pain.

"I can't rightly say, child. It appears they meant to help. It's some old way, maybe, to prevent or cure lameness. It's hard to say."

That night we did not mind our "slim fare"; we ate only a little of the pinto beans cooked with salt pork. We ate in silence and went silently to bed.

The next day Grandfather rode Dip southwest for ten miles to buy a horse from a rancher by the name of Cronin, who accepted the last of Grandfather's "nest egg," his treasured insurance against disaster, and a personal note for the balance, after harvest. The horse was cheaper than most because he was a poor horse. When Papa saw him, he told Grandfather he had been cheated. The horse's name was Bugs as the Cronin family had decided that he was "a little crazy." Bugs was much smaller than Dip, his ribs showed, his hip bones were sharp, he carried his head down as if in perpetual depression, and his ears showed no spirit. But he had a long silky mane and tail, and his dark-bay hide was like velvety fur. His appearance was forlorn but his legs were short and strong. Bugs was a bundle of contradictions.

"If you're going to keep him," Papa said, "we'll feed him up and give him good care so he'll take some pride in himself and hold his head up. It looks awful to see a horse hang his head like that."

"We had to have one quick and cheap who would work. Cronin says he's broke to harness and he's a good worker."

"Well," Papa said, "there's something wrong with this horse."

"Cronin was honest. He said Bugs is a little off."

"He has been mistreated as a colt," Papa said. "His spirit is broken, or he hasn't been fed right, or maybe he didn't have any real quality to start with." He patted Bugs' neck and ran his hand gently down his nose and over his muzzle, but the little horse did

not respond. He was a new challenge, a new bond for Papa,
Grandfather, and me. Each of us longed to help Bugs, to restore
him, to lift his spirits and his head.

"Let's hitch them up and go to the creek for our water first
thing in the morning; the barrels are about empty. I think Dip
likes the poor devil all right."

19

THE NEXT MORNING at dawn, before going to the creek for water, the men hitched Dip and Bugs to the doubletrees and walked them out to where Fred lay dead. Bugs snorted and flattened his ears. Dip whinnied and reared and tried to break free. After quieting the fearful horses, the men secured Fred's great stiff body with ropes and chains and dragged him a mile away into a draw.

"It's a wonder the coyotes didn't try to eat him in the night," Mama said.

I ran to the barn and cried, and cried more when I saw the long white hairs from his mane, hardly noticed before, caught in the rough boards of the stall. Bounce came in and nudged me, then stood back, his tail down, wagging slowly to express his sympathy.

We left the barn and walked into the field. Our broomcorn was higher than my head. The rising sunlight filtered down through the green blades, the field was fragrant with morning. A grasshopper flew onto my dress. He looked at me, his eyes direct and impertinent, as if he knew everything I did not. Then he spat his "tobacco juice": his comment on my grief in the natural world of so much birthing, hatching, eating, dying.

When the men returned and hitched the horses to the wagon for their trip to the creek for water, I waited until they drove out the gate before Bounce and I ran after them. The spicy fragrance of sage was in the air. Soapweeds, as we called yucca, had lost their creamy blooms. In the spring Grandfather had showed me the moth that pollinates the yuccas and taught me the parts of the flowers.

"No accident, either," he said. "That moth has a special kind of mouth for gathering yucca pollen off the stamen. She carries it to another yucca flower and takes great care to place it just where it belongs on the stigma. In 1872 a Professor Riley found that out. I read about it and never forgot it because it just goes to show there's a pattern. Pull a few threads and you undo nature's pattern. Understand?"

"What if she goes to another kind of flower?" I asked.

"She doesn't. She and the yucca can't live without each other. You see, when she lays her eggs in the seed capsules, she has already provided her children with food by pollination for the new seeds. And there's plenty of seed for her young and for new yuccas, too."

I wanted very much to know how the insect knew to do this, but all Grandfather could say was, "That's Nature." The number of Nature's secrets multiplied; sometimes it seemed to me that we were more ignorant than the creatures and plants.

The prairie dog town we passed on our way to the creek provided such entertainment that momentarily I forgot my sorrow. In summer these gay little marmots spent the hot afternoons in their burrows, coming out to search for food in the mornings and late afternoons. They ate seeds and grass, the good buffalo grass that was highly nutritious the year round, even when it was brown and dry. The water in these was all they needed. Fat and furry, their cheek pouches full, hundreds were feeding, each close to his mound of earth tunneled from the ground. Posted sentinels sat up on their hind legs, their bright, intelligent eyes watching our approach to determine if we were among their enemies—coyotes, badgers, eagles, and hawks. In the fall, rattlesnakes sometimes moved into abandoned holes, often forcing the abandonment. Among the prairie dogs a jackrabbit was feeding, his fur blending with the dun summer grass, only his long ears moving. Suddenly Bounce sprang into the town after the "jack," who leaped into the air and ran in great bounds, quickly outdistancing the dog. He stopped abruptly, sat up and looked back, then ran on. At this commotion, the prairie dog sentinels gave their shrill warning call. The quick little animals sped to their burrows, sat up for an instant to sound the alarm, and with a flick of their short tails, they dove into the earth. They must have turned about at once for heads appeared for a cautious glance, then they sprang back onto their mounds, looked all about and returned to their feeding, or comic antics, leaving the watch to their sentries. Through all this they appeared quick and bold and cheerful. When really frightened, as by a rattlesnake taking over his burrow, the little prairie dog stood his ground and chattered in outraged protest, before he bowed to the inevitable. Then he accepted his dispossession and dug himself another home, deep, with many side chambers, forming the unearthed dirt into a flood-proof mound.

The rangy jackrabbit that had escaped stopped under a sagebrush and continued his feeding. Unlike the cottontail, it was not his habit to seek safety in a hole.

At the creek the horses were freed to drink and rest under the cottonwoods while Grandfather and Papa filled the barrels with cold, clean water. Bounce and I waded in the shallow stream, he playfully trying to catch minnows.

I came out of the water to talk to Bugs, who did not respond.

"We'll kill him with kindness," Papa called.

I thought of Fred, so responsive, and it seemed to me that Dip was thinking of him too, for he stood with lowered head, now and then giving a great sigh. I pressed my face against his warm neck to hide my renewing tears.

"None of that," Grandfather scolded. "We'll rest a spell," he said to Papa, and came over to me, thumping my shoulder with his knuckles. "You are ordinarily a cheerful girl. Now, you will just have to get used to Nature's ways."

"I hate Nature's ways!"

"Well, you are one of them. And let me tell you, little miss, 'hate' is bad medicine. You'll do well to think that over."

"But I love Fred!"

"If you will stop these infernal tears"—Grandfather lowered his voice, which was already low—"I may go on a little jaunt tonight, and you may go with me."

20

So at last I was permitted to go for a night walk with Grandfather. When he opened the door, the light from our room in the earth leaped into the dark, and we with it; when he closed the door, the light was pressed back as into a box. We stood in the night. I saw nothing in that blackness, but I heard the horses in the barn nosing the hay, blowing against their lips with a peaceful rippling sound.

Grandfather did not go through the west gate but struck off across the cane patch to the south. The cane was tall and cool. Walking along the rows, brushing against the crisp leaves, smelling the cane's green fragrance, I knew my way. Field mice squeaked and ran, their feet making small soft sounds. Bounce followed stealthily although he had been forbidden this particular jaunt. At the fence, Grandfather stepped on the lowest barbed wire and held the middle one up for me to go through, then he half-stepped, half-leaped over the top wire.

Our eyes had grown used to the dark; the dark had a sheen

from the stars. Ahead, Grandfather walked as if to a destination, the sound of his long steps guiding me. Bounce stayed close at my heels and I was glad. I was not afraid of the night; I liked being in it, but this was no ordinary walk. I had wondered all summer about these night walks and now felt a sense of promise and portent. The moon slid up fast from another region, revealing the straight horizon a world away. Black shadows appeared beside the scattered sage and soapweeds, but the big plain lay under the moonlight in opal clarity.

Walking was easier now. I could see the grass-blades and the tough little weeds resting from the day's wind. Grandfather had told me they were not resting but growing: "Plants do their growing at night." I stopped to watch a milkweed grow, but nothing was disclosed to me beyond an exchange of affection. The scent of skunk drifted by, refined by distance. Bounce lifted his dog nose into the air current but did not leave me. Because of our loitering, Grandfather was far ahead, and we ran to catch up, avoiding the prickly-pear cactus that grew in clumps of runners close to the ground, its thick oval leaves dangerous with thorns that pierced and ached the flesh, as I knew from experience.

Grandfather's lean frame cast a long black shadow. I watched my own and the dog's shadow gliding along. Bounce and I sensed our privilege to this journey depended upon our making no sounds other than our breath and the soft pad of our feet. We were following someone we loved, but we were drawn nearer to each other in the wake of that tall man's solitude.

We had been walking toward the part of the creek where we bathed and from which we hauled water. There the banks sloped gently down to the stream where horses and wagons forded the shallow water. Willows and cottonwoods lined the shore, and wild onions and red sand poppies grew there. Kildeers ran crying bleakly, and bats flew at dusk. But Grandfather veered off to the southeast where there were no trails, past a prairie dog town of many mounds. The little bushy-tailed rodents were asleep in their burrows, but here and there a small billy owl sat on the mound of an abandoned hole he had taken for his home. Once we surprised a large badger on his night hunt, and Grandfather turned with a sharp command to Bounce. In a fight the badger could have torn Bounce apart with his sharp claws, but he chose to dig rapidly into the earth, ignoring us. Farther along we saw three coyotes relaying in pursuit of a jackrabbit. After that the plain seemed deserted except for occasional small rustlings and the running of small feet.

There was nothing in sight on the open prairie. The high clear air shimmered with moonlight. The silence deepened into a sound of itself, a palpable atmosphere through which we walked to what destination I did not know. In this unpeopled place what destination could there be? An intensely felt but not understood part of me was being stretched in every direction to the circular horizon and upward to that immense field of stars. I was aware of my hunger then, a hunger that stirred me to living life, a knowledge that I was more than myself, that self of the hours of day and night, that the unknown answer lay all about me, that everything spoke to me and yet I could not understand. I wanted to be alone with this new feeling, but I was overcome with such a loneliness that I dared to run ahead and slip my hand into Grandfather's. His dry fingers bent to enclose my hand that sought his finite touch and comfort. We walked like this until we neared the length of prairie that broke off at a precipice, a long high cliff following the creekbed far below. He let go my hand and walked more slowly, scuffing over the grass here and there, feeling for button cactus. He sat down, raised his knees, and let his arms rest upon them. A sigh came out of his slackened body. He motioned for me to sit near him and for Bounce to lie down at his feet. We sat looking into the nothingness of night. We listened to baby coyotes yipping over a kill their parents had brought them.

I supposed that soon we would continue our ramble or turn back, and found nothing unusual in Grandfather's silence as he rarely spoke unless he had something particular and necessary to say. I did not pester him with questions when he was "studying about things," as he called serious thinking.

Bounce whined very low and started up.

"Down!" Grandfather said in a hushed voice. Bounce obeyed reluctantly, pressing against my bare legs. I pulled him back across my lap, keeping my fingers in his thick coat. He was trembling, wanting to whine or bark, but he understood his master's command.

"There's a horse!" I could not help my exclamation as a young bay trotted up near us out of nowhere.

Grandfather turned his head and looked at me in rather a sur-

prised way, but he was not at all surprised by the horse. Then
he did a strange thing. He nodded a thoughtful yes. I did not
know what he meant. We turned back to watching the horse.

"Let him be," Grandfather said. "That's Daft."

"Who is Daft?" I whispered.

"Never mind now."

Daft was a dark bay with the short head of the mustang. His
coat gleamed in the moonlight as if his owner curried him every
day and combed out his long black mane and tail. He was very
frisky. Apparently he had been grazing and suddenly felt an urge
to play. He nipped a little grass, then capered about, arching his
neck, kicking his hind legs out, stopping dead still, then throwing
his head back and smelling the air with pleasure. It was great fun
to watch him, and I knew that Grandfather had brought me to
share his entertainment. I wondered for a moment how on this
vast plain Grandfather knew exactly where to find Daft at his
summer-night play. We had crossed no fences but our own, we
had seen no lighted windows or farmhouse, but farms were distant
from one another and I had not expected to see one. This walk
proved once again how well Grandfather knew this unmarked
land.

Bounce was trembling more and whining under his breath as if
he would burst if not allowed to run and bark. I held him and
stroked his head, but he was not consoled.

Daft whinnied. Grandfather said, "Hear that?"

"Yes."

"Well, I'll declare."

Suddenly, I saw Daft's forelegs curve, his black hoofs lift, and
he galloped away in his own thunder, his mane and tail flying
beautifully. He ran in utmost delight, swerved back, and raced
by us at frightening speed, swiping us with a stream of cold night
air. He was running toward the cliff. We leaped up. At the last
dangerous moment, he stopped short with legs stiffened, braking
his motion.

"Thank God!" Grandfather said. He touched me. "Let's go
home now."

At once Daft galloped away over the plain, farther this time,
and thundered back in the direction of the cliff. Grandfather put
an arm around my shoulders and tried to press my face against
his side, but I pulled away. Bounce jerked free of my hand and

ran after the horse, barking madly. Daft streaked past us like a cold wind, ears back, nostrils wide open, and his eyes wild. He headed straight for the precipice. Beyond it, suspended for an instant in the empty air, he fell, screaming all the way down. The horror of an echo came back to us from the rock wall of the cliff.

In the awesome quiet after, we waited stunned, and then I began to cry for Daft.

"I'm sorry, child. I brought you just to see Daft play."

We began our anguished long walk home. Grandfather let me cry awhile, to comfort me, and when I could listen to him, he said, "Don't cry anymore, don't grieve, and I'll try and tell you why. Daft is all right. We'll come back again and you'll see."

"No! How can I see him again when he is killed?"

"I can't very well explain that when I don't know myself. There are many strange things we don't yet understand, but that doesn't mean you need to be afraid of something you don't understand, does it?"

"I guess not."

"Then I'll tell you this. I wanted to see if *you* could see Daft. You saw him first. Now Daft ran over that cliff and killed himself two years ago. I felt mighty bad. Daft was my horse, my favorite, but he got to eating locoweed and he was ruined."

"Was he loco?"

"Yes, he was loco. I didn't know it at first, and I named him Daft because he acted so daft."

"I know about locoweed."

"But we don't know all the rest. After Daft was killed, I had only one horse for a time, and one day I rode over to see an artesian well come in, and I rode home after dark. That was the first time I saw Daft. It scared me, I can tell you, but I got over that. I've seen that horse many times. I'd walk over there on fair nights just to watch him play. He hardly ever jumps off the cliff. He just plays. I thought he had quit doing that or I wouldn't have taken you there."

"I might go again," I said.

"We'll talk about that later."

"I'd like to see him because he isn't real."

"That's the pure self of Daft," he said.

I was bewildered by this, but Grandfather said, "Never mind," so I knew he was talking to himself.

"Little Cheyenne Riding Like the Wind," he said as if he were still talking with himself, but I knew he was appealing to me. "I am going to take you into my confidence. You understand that?"

"Yes."

"I have told no one about seeing Daft, but several others have seen him too. I just keep still."

"Why?"

"Because I don't understand it, and I don't like talking a lot of nonsense. Therefore, I am asking you to keep this a secret with me."

"Even from Mama and Papa?"

"Yes."

"I promise." I felt proud and glad that he trusted me and wished me to share such a marvelous secret.

After that we walked in silence, and I longed for the sound of Daft's screaming to go out of my head. I wanted to go again if I could be sure that he would not jump off the precipice. I couldn't bear it again. I was thinking so hard about all that had happened that I stumbled and fell against Bounce. He growled, and he had never growled at me before. I got to my feet, and there was Daft standing a little way off looking at us in a peaceful, browsing way. I began to shudder, and no matter how gently his large dark eyes looked at me, my skin was cold with terror and I felt all my pores rise. It was almost impossible to take my gaze away, but I made the effort to lift my face toward Grandfather. He was smiling at the pure self of Daft.

"Thank you, lad," Grandfather said to him, and the terror let go my body.

I noticed our shadows lying on the grass and cautiously slid my gaze along the ground where Daft's legs and black hoofs stood firm and solid. I saw the fetlock tuft of hair. There was no shadow for Daft. He stood free in his own image, resplendent in the moon's bright light, free of the bright moon's shade.

Daft was so real I ran to touch him, to show him my joy and relief, but as I reached out my hand, he disappeared. He did not run away, he simply was not there.

"But where—?"

"Now, now, be glad Daft came back to show you he is still about and not below the cliff."

"Have you seen his bones there?"

"Yes, I have seen his bones there."

"Then—?"

"You will have to accept Daft's ways just as he has to accept yours."

The thought that Daft would have to accept my ways occupied me for much of the way home.

"Cheyenne—" Grandfather pointed to the three black shapes sliding over the grass beside us. "I am surprised you didn't notice that Daft cast no shadow."

"I did."

"Well, don't be afraid. I am not afraid. Daft is not afraid. So you need not be afraid. Is that clear?"

"Yes."

"We are privileged to see him." Grandfather gave my shoulder his bony, affectionate tap.

"Bounce was afraid," I said.

"I can't answer for Bounce. What interests me is that Bounce saw Daft."

Bounce, his tail now lifted high from between his shivering legs, wandered ahead of us in his customary good humor. We were all a part of the luminous night, Grandfather, myself, Bounce, and Daft.

21

Our broomcorn matured without mishap of prairie fire or drouth. There were days of scorching winds and fierce sun when it seemed that the crop would burn up, but the fertile soil had stored its winter moisture well. The great snows and even the blizzard that had imprisoned us underground had secured our harvest. From the appearance of the first green blades, Papa walked in the field on Sundays observing the growth.

But one Sunday we all had the pleasure of a day spent on the farm of Carrie and Jim Whitehead. There, water, as much a miracle as a ripe crop, ran in garden ditches; little ducks swam in a ditch near the windmill; lemon yellow chicks followed mother hens; a cow and her calf dozed in the barnyard; horses grazed in the pasture. It was a simple farm but it provided well for their needs. They had built it gradually by hard work and "doing without." Carrie had sawed and hammered together her own kitchen table and cupboards. Their great wisdom was that they had put

their cash into digging a well. Papa had foolishly wasted his by
buying land when there was land free for the homesteading. Since
he had done this on his father's impractical advice, and paid for
Grandfather's few farm implements about to be repossessed, he
blamed him for our extreme poverty when he was not in the mood
to blame himself.

A big surprise at the Whiteheads' was their young son, Dale,
Marcy's age. Mama and Papa knew of him, but somehow in the
seclusion of our lives this good fact had been missed, or concealed: He was a son. Dale and Marcy, after a wary, intuitive
appraisal, began to play together. He was a generous little boy
eager to show and share his interests. A small herd of flat tin
cattle was his favorite possession. At the end of a "cattle drive" he
said, "Here, Marshy, you can take her home," and handed Marcy
a pretty Jersey cow. That tin cow was her cherished toy for the
next two years.

After midday dinner, the men lounged on the back porch and
toured the barnyard, talking of crops and animals. Mama and
Carrie, so hungry for company, talked all through dish-washing.
They took off their long aprons and sat at the kitchen table, continuing their exchange of problems, serious or sad, or laughing
together like young girls. Dale and Marcy and I were given permission to play out of doors, where we watched the clear water
sparkle in the ditches like a magic carpet under the tiny ducks.
Fresh vegetables in the garden were as exciting to us as candy in
the glass case at Tullery's store. We longed for a well of our own
with a windmill wheeling the wind, creaking in the great silence.

In late August our broomcorn was ripe enough to pull, and I was
tall enough to reach the broom. I had seen it growing from seed
and I wanted to take part in the harvest. Too, I was needed.
Every hand was needed. Grandfather showed me how to take hold
of the stalk with my left hand, grip the broom with my right,
and quickly break it free. He, Mama, Papa, and I each took a
row, and as I could not keep up, Papa, who was a fast puller, now
and then "caught me up." Marcy tagged after Papa, playing along
under the hot, crackling shade of the broomcorn. We left the
brush to cure, in small piles along the rows. Jim Whitehead was
able to help us the second day, and on the third morning Cooper

Loveland rode into our yard, unsaddled his horse, Bo, and turned him loose.

"He won't go no place without me," he said. "Will you, Bo?" The horse nuzzled the young cowboy. "I saw these two women working in the field, and since this country here is awful low on population, I figured I'd offer my services. I've pulled when I was a kid."

Papa was pleased, but he said, "Cooper, I can't hire anybody and you're a cowboy; how would I pay you back?"

"I'm not looking for pay or payback, Walt. Just kinda want to pull broomcorn and rest Bo awhile."

"Well, now—" Papa said. "This is hard work and I sure appreciate it. I'll find a way to—"

Cooper looked at Mama and said, "Maybe she can figure out something." His high-cheekboned face was impassive, but later Mama said he had a tender look.

"I think I can; I'll try."

The tall young man moved away from Papa to speak to Mama in confidence. The humor in his black eyes and the whole sincere look of his face and body spoke in his favor.

"We figure on getting married. I just filed my claim on a homestead." He smiled and added wryly, "Her folks say she has to marry land."

Mama's romanticism, repressed by our hard life, bubbled like an underground spring that had found a new outlet. She smiled into Cooper's face, now reddened to include his ears, and said something that astounded him.

"Cooper Loveland, thank you!"

"How's *that?*" he asked.

"Oh, nothing—it's just that—well, it's just that I'm glad!"

"Thank you, Mrs. Babb. I wish her folks felt the same."

"They will—in time."

"I mean them to—in time."

"I am dying to tell Carrie and Jim. May I?"

"I'm afraid not. We're going to have to run away."

"Oh, good!"

Cooper frowned.

"Oh, don't frown. Maxine will like running away."

Cooper shook his head, puzzled, but his eyes were laughing.

"You ladies! You're all as wild as little fillies. Begging your pardon, Mrs. Babb."

Mama became serious. "Cooper Loveland, I hope you won't put too tight a rein on Maxine."

"That I won't. I don't want to gentle her too much."

"She's full of fun," Mama said. "I used to be, too."

"Mrs. Babb." Cooper stopped. "Would you like to run away with us, kinda chaperone Maxine?"

"Oh, for heaven's sake, no. You don't need me. Run away, go on a honeymoon to Colorado Springs or someplace! When you start homesteading . . ."

"Colorado Springs," Cooper said slowly, "Say, that's an idea."

"It will give you and Maxine some good memories to talk about for years on these lonesome plains."

"I never talked so much in my whole life, I better get to the point. Will you give me a note inviting the girls here next Friday evening? I'll put it in the mailbox. Only Maxine will walk down. I'll be here. We won't be a nuisance. Doc Burtis wants to drive out and check up on you, then he wants to drive us to Lamar and witness us. He thinks this might soften the folks a bit. Doc has a new Ford, wants a long drive, I think. Well, we could go from Lamar by train to Colorado Springs for a week or so." For Cooper, this was a long speech. He sighed.

"I'll write the note now before we go to the field."

Mama skipped down into the dugout and came out shortly with the note. Cooper put it carefully in his shirt pocket. We all went into the field together and started on our rows.

Cooper outpulled even Papa, and all he said the whole morning was, "Have to get in practice to be a sodbuster."

22

WITH THE HELP OF NEIGHBORS, we pulled the broomcorn, and it lay in small piles along the rows curing for a few days. At pulling and seeding time there was a general exchange of labor among the distant farms. Men and women enjoyed a release from isolation and loneliness in the hard shared work and the big meals usually served in yards on new pine planks resting on sawhorses. Seats were long planks supported by nail kegs and lard cans. Because timber was scarce, these makeshift tables and benches were shared from farm to farm.

Mama's good friend Carrie came to help her with the cooking. Grandfather had to build a fire outdoors because our tiny two-lid monkey stove was not up to harvest meals. Marcy and Dale and I were kept busy gathering cow chips from the free range. This dried dung burned fast, but the big herds had been grazing west of us, leaving plenty of fuel. As the food was served, my job was to move about, waving a dish towel over the table to keep the flies away. Men washed at the bench beside the dugout and came to the table with sunburned, soap-shined faces, wet hair, and clean work-hardened hands. Wives had saved bacon and salt pork grease all summer, cooked it up with lye, and made soap for harvesttime as well as for washing clothes.

A few days after the broomcorn was pulled, a neighbor drove along the rows while Papa and Grandfather and two other home-steaders stacked the small piles onto a flatbed wagon. I carried drinking water, in a gallon jug wrapped in wet gunnysack, to the men, and rode on the wagon until it was back even with the dugout. Rattlesnakes liked to nap under the piles and the men, working fast, often forgot the danger. Just after I had climbed onto the wagon, one of the men picked up a pile of broomcorn, snake and all, and was preparing to throw it onto the wagon when he saw the rattler. In his quick effort not to throw the snake toward me, he fell backward, still clutching the deadly bundle of brooms and snake. The snake was rattling his tail in warning and writhing into a coil from which he could strike. The man was on the ground. The rattler, by nature nervous, aggressive, was in panic; his eyes glinted, his forked tongue slithered rapidly back and forth, his flat head, with its poison-filled fangs ready, darted toward a target. The men were shouting, "Look out! Look out!" The horses were rearing and snorting in terror. Papa kicked the snake and the broomcorn away from the man, who sprang to his feet. The rattler, still fearful and angry, coiled and would have struck at the man but for a dry clod thrown by Papa.

"That comes from pitching baseball," Papa boasted.

The rattlesnake slid away into the field too swiftly to be harmed.

"We've got to watch out now, fellows; he's probably under another pile already."

This reminded the man who had nearly been bitten of another experience. Rattlesnakes had struck his five horses as they grazed. Their heads had swollen to enormous size.

"My wife and son and myself rubbed them with coal oil all night long, and, by Jove, we saved our horses."

"Plague on the dang rattlesnakes and sidewinders!" Grandfather said. "They put the fear of death in every living creature except the roadrunner. I wish that little old desert bird lived here. Now, I never kill a useful snake, but I'll tell you—" He looked up at me, still shaken. "Best you stay out of the field until we can see all around us."

"Next morning," the man went on with his story, "me and my boy and two, three neighbors spread out and killed I don't know how many rattlers, a lot just born, ten or twelve to a litter, I reckon you call it. We'd a lost all our stock, they was so thick. You know, a funny thing, a mother snake don't care a hang about her children. Soon as they're born, or hatched out, as the case may be, they got to look after themselves, and by dang, they can do it. You have to give 'em credit."

At the west end of the field near the road, the men laid down a base of broomcorn stalks for a long narrow rick and began stacking the brooms from both sides, heads in and butts out, to protect them from a rare but possible rain. The crop had to cure for six to eight weeks in the ricks.

"The seeds have got to sweat first for two or three weeks," Grandfather told Papa. "Seeds sweat. Now the greener we can cure this straw, the higher price we'll get. Look at the best brooms next time you go to the store."

"I'll do that." Papa didn't relish being taught before the other men. "First time I ever raised broomcorn. First time at dryland farming, too. I lived where it rains."

The men did not ask him if he had farmed. Some of them were new at it, too, when they came out to homestead.

In the lull until seeding time, Papa and Grandfather helped others pull and stack their broomcorn. Mama helped the wives; children did chores and played. A farmer near Springfield by the name of Van Houten, simply called "Dutch," owned a seeder and baler and went from farm to farm. When our turn came, the distant neighbors came again to help. However crude this operation, it was effective, and it was enchanting to Marcy and me. Men carried broomcorn stalks from the ricks to the seeder, which was mainly a large turning cylinder with spikes. They held onto the stalks, never letting go, turning them until all the seeds had fallen away. From there, they placed them in the baler, again with the brooms in for protection, the butts out, trying to make each bale weigh five hundred pounds. What we liked most about this was to watch the Dutchman's mare, Tulip, do her own job perfectly. This was to walk around in a circle pulling the wires to tighten and press the brooms together into a bale.

"Tulip knows just when to stop; she knows when the bale is just tight enough," Van Houten said in an accent we liked, an accent that made English sound innocently appealing.

We had sixteen bales. Soon a buyer came from Kansas City and went to all the farms pricing and contracting. We received fifty dollars a ton delivered to Holly, forty miles away. Papa dreamed of a larger crop next year and a better price.

On the strength of the crop, he bought a wagon and a team of mares, Katy and Buff. Katy was a dark bay with black mane and tail. Buff was black with white stockings and a star on her forehead. It was clear from the first day that Katy and Papa didn't get along. When he stung her with a line for being stubborn, she waited her chance and tried to bite his arm.

Grandfather smiled to himself. "You'll never get the best of that lady, son. She is as spirited as Carrie Mayo Whitehead. You'll have to learn ways to get around her."

"I'm damned if I will," Papa said. Katy was equally determined.

With Papa and Grandfather going off to Holly, Mama, Marcy, and I were to be alone a week. And if Old Loony did not walk by to frighten us again, the absence of the men from our crowded room was not unwelcome. Aside from work, we planned a walk to Carrie's and anticipated a certain freedom from the routine that the good presence of men required. With them home, we felt the ease of their protection and the quiet joy of looking after their comfort. But with them away, we delighted in a changed rhythm of living and a brief flowering of our very own ways. Mama said, "Now we can breathe freely." But when Papa kissed her good-bye and we watched him and Grandfather drive out the gate, her eyes filled with tears.

The load was pulled by the two teams, Katy and Buff hitched ahead of Dip and Bugs. Five bales to a load meant more trips or further neighbor cooperation. The trip required two and a half days each way, so the men went for a week. They delivered their crops, bought coal and feed, and drove back over the autumn cool plains with a sense of pride in their year's work and a feeling of gratitude to a land and its climate that tried hard in most years to reject them.

Seven days later, in the clear, high silence, we heard the sounds of wagons from a long distance. Bounce took off down the road with yelps of joy. That morning we had walked twice to the creek and carried back as much water as we could for both men and horses. The barn was clean. The dugout was fragrant with simmering pinto beans and with corn pone made in a skillet since the stove had no oven. We changed our dresses, combed our hair, and walked to the gate to welcome our men. They were in good spirits from their time away, the sale of their crop, and doubtless from their own brief liberty from us. Our eyes, and perhaps our hearts, looked freshly at one another.

Carrie's brother, Curtis, just behind Papa and Grandfather, stopped his team to bring Marcy and me gifts: two little brooms. Marcy began at once to sweep the bare ground around the dugout door. We were so pleased with our brooms that Papa withheld his gifts for us till the evening: two small iron banks—for Marcy, an iron horse; for me, a safe. Grandfather gave us each ten pennies, which we deposited and rattled in pride of our wealth.

"It's earned," he said, sticking to his principle not to spoil us. "For pulling broomcorn."

"I didn't pull," Marcy said, honest, worried.

"For driving the horses, then."

"As soon as the horses are rested," Papa said, "we'll have to go to the cedars for wood. I don't want any of you far from the dugout. We saw big gray wolves today; some of them will weigh a hundred and seventy or eighty pounds, big fellows!"

"Now, now," Grandfather said. "They'd have to be awful hungry to attack a person; though they did back me all the way home one fierce winter. They probably didn't know what I was. They're afraid of people now, and moving out."

"All the same, it'd scare Ginny and the girls just to see them."

"We might walk to Carrie's again," Mama said quietly.

"Well, watch out for that Banter bull," Papa said.

"That's more like it," Grandfather said. "But you'll be safe. It's better not to borrow trouble."

"Well, girls," Papa said, "we're all going to town Saturday. I want to pay our grocery bill at Tullery's store. Write some letters, Ginny, and tell everybody about our crop. I'll buy you a handful of stamps."

23

We had raised a crop, paid our bills, and had only a few coins left. The winter was almost as hard as the first one except that the hardships were not new.

One year so like the first and then another went by, and yet in all those days and nights none was the same. Every sunrise and every sunset was resplendent in its own way. The sun at horizon, mornings and evenings, relumed the powerful being of that harsh and silent land. Its great hush was deepened by the longing, mournful mating call of gray wolves in the nights of spring; the undulating whir of insects in the summer dark; the wild geese flying north and south; the howling winter winds. The meadowlark sang its joyous song. Mockingbirds, hawks, and owls. A wildcat scream. A coyote lament. Wind. Wind. A wild, lonesome land. And still we stayed. It laid its claim on our deepest mind while we but claimed its earth.

The winters passed slowly, the summers more quickly. The summers of cool nights, hot windy days with frequent electric

storms that brought no rain. Spring and summer were filled with
orderly work in the fields, work that twice came to nothing.
Broomcorn shriveled up and died before it could grow; the acres
that grew burned up in the fields, victims of sun without rain.

"This country is no good!" Papa shouted in terrible frustration.

Grandfather answered him calmly, defending it. "All it needs
is water. The soil is virgin and rich. Grass is good for stock all
year round."

"All it needs is water," Papa mocked him. "We can't get ahead
enough to buy stock to eat the grass!"

"Our horses graze; and you added to the barn for Katy and
Buff."

"Some barn! Cedar logs hauled all the way from the eastern
slope of the Rockies and a lot of our corn and cane fodder wired
down for a roof."

"It serves. It's warm."

"I can't even raise my own seed!"

We had matured enough cane and maize for the horses; and a
few potatoes and pinto beans. But we were desperate for water.

"I'm danged if I can eat another bean," Grandfather said.

And Papa, somewhat restored in belief, said, "Then, here, Dad,
take three or four."

Mama often ate less so that Marcy and I could have more, and
even the more was not much. The pure air must have fed us all.
We were thin and often hungry, but we worked and were not ill.
We were still ignorant of edible weeds save the young Russian
thistle, and there were no Indians or native grandmothers to teach
us. Carrie showed us the cleansing lamb's-quarter and poisonous
dock. Grandfather Alonzo dug up the deadly Jimsonweed or night-
shade, which could cause our horses an agonizing death, and the
familiar locoweed, which could damage their brains and vision,
causing delirium and death, if the horses were not cured by a
long and careful diet. We made sage tea for medicinal use, but
there our knowledge ended.

We suspected Bugs of loco addiction and disease and gave him
special care. He was thin, slow-gaited, and curiously unresponsive
still, but he began to raise his head and favor us with a few signs
of recognition. His troubles were not from loco, but whatever
they were, they disappeared the second year, and patient Dip's
workmate became a friendly and humorous little horse.

Papa favored dignified, quiet Buff, and continued to quarrel with Katy, who fought back with head jerks, crowding, and enough sly movements to cause him to keep away from her hind-quarters. She was gentle with Marcy and me.

Once when we had to buy grain for the horses, Papa said with apology, "We have to take good care of the horses first. They work."

"We've been playing and didn't have sense enough to know it," Mama said, but she was smiling, and we all understood about the horses.

What really upset Mama was to run out of coffee and be too hard up to buy any. Whenever her mother sent a one-dollar bill, she debated whether to buy coffee or writing paper and stamps. As much as she liked to write letters, she usually decided in favor of coffee.

"We can't often get to town in winter to mail letters, anyway. I'll write only to Mom."

Coffee meant something more to her than a hot drink. Now and then in the afternoon she sat for awhile in a fresh apron, slowly drinking warmed-over breakfast coffee, her face passive, her gaze rapt in faraway memories or in dreams of escape. She did not mind the hard work, only the terrible loneliness. In that solitary rite she reached backward or forward to friends, perhaps, or simply retired within herself to renew her forces.

"Your mother has the blues," Papa explained when Mama drank two cups of coffee.

At this infringement of her privacy, Mama, so even-tempered and agreeable, then rose and began some work, saying, "Oh, for heaven's sake, a person can't even have the blues!"

I became a great respecter of *the blues*. They suggested mysteries beneath the surface, questions that could only be thought about, not spoken.

Occasionally Papa behaved as if he were alone among us, whistling to himself, his big smile or his quick anger no evident part of him. Then we knew that he also had the blues.

When Grandfather went for a long tramp over the plains, or sat on his wire cot playing a sad old song through a piece of paper folded over a comb, we guessed he had the blues, especially if the song were one about "wandering over this wide, weary world."

In our small, crowded room, each managed to achieve an occasional moment of desperately needed privacy called the blues.

The next spring Grandfather bought seed on time, and we planted again. Our crops grew past their first green days, into summer, bearing full heads of feterita and maize, long full brushes of broomcorn; and south of the dugout our cane grew tall and sweet. We walked every day in the fields watching for the moment of ripeness, to harvest and dry our crops before frost. If we walked there, we appeased the hostile sun, the treacherous sky. Mama and Papa talked; they saw our bills paid at Tullery's and the feed and seed store. They spoke of imaginary orders from the catalog because we were patched ragged. Papa bought a new plowshare. We all dreamed of a cow and chickens.

When the broomcorn was ripe, the four of us went into the field and pulled it. Marcy, now seven, was sweeping the yard around the dugout door. Bounce, told to stay there, was watching. We would head maize and chop cane while the broomcorn was curing.

The first afternoon, when we had covered only a small part of the large field, thunderheads began forming and grew dark with rain and agitated by wind. The horses, grazing on the range, laid back their ears, ran about, and kicked in sheer pleasure. Lightning quivered for a time, then flashed in long spears, and thunder sounded in violent claps and long low rolls.

"It may not do a thing but flash and roar," Papa said, "but we'd better go in till it's over."

Large drops of rain fell, and the warm air cooled.

"Godalmighty! It's going to hail!"

We ran.

The horses were running through the open gate toward the barn. By the time we reached the dugout, marbles of ice pelted us. Marcy ran to grasp Papa's hand. The hailstones were growing larger and we took shelter on the dugout steps to watch through the open door. The hail struck the hard ground and leaped about; the hailstones were now almost the size of chicken eggs. The roof groaned. The maize and the broomcorn began to fall.

"If it isn't too bad, it will rise up in a couple of days of sun," Grandfather said. "I've seen it do that."

"It's all down," Papa said. "It's *down*." His voice was flat and stony.

The hail kept falling. The strong plants resisted, swayed as if dodging, were struck again and again. The whole field went down. The cane, only bent and torn, was leaning, but it would stand again.

The hail stopped abruptly. Light spread through the darkened sky. Clouds broke and sailed away on high wind currents. The sun was still hidden. The cold air was growing warm again. Hailstones were white on the fields and yard.

We stepped into the open. Papa looked far out over the ruined acres. Tears streamed down his tanned face. He had not cried since the loss of his son.

Grandfather saw and went to the barn.

Papa placed an arm around Mama's shoulders but he still looked out over the fields. After awhile he said, "We'll try it once more next spring. We can't fail every year."

"But what if we should?" Mama asked in despair.

"Well, if we don't make it then, we'll be starved out; we'll have to find a town." He glanced at me, then turned back to Mama. "Maybe we ought to go to Elkhart this fall. It's just over the state line in western Kansas. The girls ought to be in school. We can come back in time to plant."

"Oh, Walt, let's go and *never* come back!"

"We'll see, Ginny. This is a good country in lots of ways. I heard about a farm on the creek we could rent next spring. It's over east, a house and farm buildings. Alfalfa and row crops. I bought a sow and pig from Clayton, the fellow who owns the farm."

"But we haven't a cent!"

"I pawned him my watch. I'll get it back. I can sell the pigs in Elkhart, or keep and raise more for sale. I've just now made up my mind. I'll get a job, work all winter, and pay off Tullery and the feed store here and be out of debt. I don't want to owe anybody. Only thing, we'll have to take the girls out of school early in the spring."

Mama said nothing. She was glad to go.

Papa said, "We want to leave Dad all the fuel we can. Say, you girls, go out every day or two from now on and gather all the cow chips you can find." He turned back to Mama. "Tullery will let me have a supply of groceries for him. Dad will be glad we're gone as soon as he gets used to it."

I felt grieved to think of leaving Grandfather Alonzo.

Papa called him from the barn. "Let's all go out and see what we have to do to save a little of this crop. See how much we can dry out and cure."

"You going to pull broomcorn lying down?" Grandfather asked, relieved to see no further tears.

"Might as well."

24

"It's a good day," Mama said. "You girls had better go out on the range and gather more cow chips. We're about out, and you're to gather a lot still for Alonzo."

The sky was clear, the wind low, the subdued sun reached us through the cold pure air of autumn. Grandfather had walked north on business of his own, letting Bounce accompany him. Papa was gathering the ruined crop for fodder. We had gone out every day; Grandfather's fuel was now a small hill in the yard. Cow chips burned fast, and Marcy and I enjoyed this frequent chore, but not today. A plenitude of chips was usually close by, but lately the cattle had been grazing far south.

I picked up two gunnysacks and called Marcy. Wherever Papa was, Marcy was. But now she came slowly from the barn as if walking in one of her fantasy games. She invited me to look into her pocket. There was a rabbit's foot.

"Where did you get that?" Papa had told us it was only a superstition about good luck. "Poor rabbit."

"If it protects us, don't tell," Marcy said. "Magic is secret."
How wonderful and necessary are magic and secrets!

Mama came up into the yard. "You must start, girls. Dark
comes early now."

I felt that presence out there; the vast plain was full of it.
There was an unspoken rule between Marcy and me that we
would never walk south alone.

"Can't we go west again?"

"Not so soon. With the big herds on the south range there'll
be more cow chips than in any other direction, and you'll get back
faster."

Old Loony's sod hut was out there too.

"Go on, sillies. It's already afternoon. I want you back by five
o'clock or I'll be worried. Watch the sun for the time."

"Old Loony might get us," Marcy said.

"Just keep a mile or two between you and his hut. You'll be a
lot nearer home than poor Old Loony's." But Mama's face revealed concern.

"What's his real name in case we should meet him?" I asked,
delaying.

"Crazy people never know their names," Marcy stated.

"Young ladies. Out there for miles and miles of godforsaken
grass, you're not likely to *meet* anybody but some white-faced
steers. This is the jumping-off place of the world!" She turned
and went down the cement steps, and I wondered if she had
forgotten that terrible day when Old Loony stopped by our gate
and stared at us on his way to town; when Bounce had crawled
on his belly and growled.

Mama's voice came up to us, and in confidence aroused by her
singing, we flung the gunnysacks over our shoulders and started
off. We walked through the beaten cane, skinned under the
barbed-wire fence, and were out on the open plain. There wasn't
another fence for miles. The little creek was two miles ahead in
a canyon. We couldn't even see the cottonwood trees along its
banks; nothing but the big plain and Old Loony's sod hut without fence or other sign of habitation. Old Loony did no farming.

The cowboy who had told Papa about the murder said that
Old Loony had only one good piece of furniture in the hut and
that was a carved box in which he kept his wife's hand. He said
years before another cowboy had observed him drying this hand,

hung on a cord in the shade for a certain period every day, the same way one would dry food.

"You know what I'd like for Christmas?" Marcy said. "A look at that dead hand."

"What a scary wish!" I said. "But if he wasn't around, I'd look."

Old Loony seldom left his hut, so far as we knew, except to walk to the distant town for supplies, but Marcy held the rabbit's foot and made a wish anyway.

No matter how we tried to edge over east or west, the plain was so large and bare that Old Loony's hut was always in front of us.

"It gives me the creeps," Marcy said. "Don't it you?"

"No," I said, full of the creeps.

It was our routine to go straight out, several miles if necessary, with our empty sacks and fill them on the way back, each day working nearer home. When we reached the place where the herds had been standing together in a storm, there were so many cakes of dry dung that we almost forgot about Old Loony. We had to watch out for cactus and dried devil's-claw, which grabbed like a hand, and particularly for rattlesnakes, which were not yet hibernating in their dens. Startled jackrabbits zigzagged away from us. Cattle grazed in the distance. We had the plain to ourselves. It was a grand feeling.

Marcy suddenly stopped. "It's time to start back." She pushed her foot against a large cow chip to loosen it from the cold earth and stooped to pick it up. "A big one right off. It's good luck." She smiled.

I glanced at the sun, harder to read in late autumn, away off to the south. "It's almost four o'clock!" Taking the first large piece of dung as a good omen and my thoughts as a charm, I said, "Let's cut over and walk back near the hut."

Marcy stared at me in alarm. "The luck is only for finding a lot of cow chips."

"We'll soon see."

Marcy hesitated, then ran after me. We gathered cow chips on the way and our sacks were full when we were within a hundred yards of Old Loony's. "It's late," Marcy warned. She was afraid of the dark, but I liked the night and told her I'd protect her. Nevertheless, Marcy reached for her rabbit's foot.

"We'll be home before dark, easy, because we're only going to walk *by* his place," I said.

When we came even with the hut, I could hear my heart beating. It felt tight like a spring. We pretended to be busy but we saw Old Loony sitting on a bench against the outside wall, watching. There was nothing to do but keep walking toward home.

Old Loony raised one hand and beckoned to us. We treated his gesture as a greeting and lifted our right hands in the salute of the plains. He rose and walked a little way toward us and called out, beckoning again.

"Don't run!" Marcy cautioned. "We're a thousand miles from a fence. You're such an idiot. I knew this would happen. With an animal it's safer just to walk. Maybe it's the same with him. We'd better just walk."

"I would like to see what *crazy* really is," I said.

"When you get home, look in the glass."

The old man hesitated and stood with his arms at his sides. He seemed puzzled at our lack of neighborliness, and I said so.

"That's just a trick," Marcy said. "They are very cunning, like foxes."

"How do you know so much all of a sudden?"

"Papa told me."

"Well, we can outrun him, don't forget."

"Don't forget he murdered his wife and cut her up."

This frightened us both.

The old man came near and said, "Howdy, girls."

"Howdy, sir."

He smiled. "I reckon I like good manners just about as much as anything."

His coarse gray hair curled like a dog's over his forehead and his bushy eyebrows shaded his old faded eyes, which watched with an animal alertness. He wore a mustache, but his whiskers were only a few days long.

I was surprised to see up close what a small man he was. His little feet stood in unlaced heavy shoes and his hands, quiet at his sides, were terrifying in their delicacy. His clothes were just ordinarily soiled and much patched. A pipe and a can of tobacco weighed down the pocket of his wool shirt. The air was growing colder and we buttoned our coats.

He glanced at the sun to judge the time, and the small sense of well-being we had begun to feel deserted us.

Old Loony said nothing. We were shy from not seeing people and also said nothing. A light gust of wind passed by and I heard the tick of grit on his shoes.

"If you're tired, come in and rest a bit."

"No, thank you," Marcy said and her voice squeaked. "We have to get home or we'll get a scolding."

He observed us slyly. "I'll show you some of my keepsakes."

We followed him; we could not resist. We leaned our sacks against the hut and went in.

The small room was neat, much like our own but less crowded. Our walls were papered with newspapers, his were bare sod. We waited stiffly near the door. My throat closed with painful shyness and I could look only at the swept dirt floor. I saw his little feet move toward the stove. He broke off two pieces of hardtack such as we ate at home and handed one to each of us.

"I would offer you girls some desert tea but I've only one cup."

"Thank you," we whispered.

"Well, I do have gourds, nice little bowls they are. But now, look here, the desert tea is mostly gone. I must gather and dry some. I am flustered by company. Haven't had company for many a year. Forget just how many."

Suddenly, in the habit of autumn, the daylight went out of the world and the plain filled with quick, rising dark. The old man closed the heavy storm door. The motion caused his clothes hanging on the back to sway ominously.

We were shut in.

"Sit down," he said and motioned toward the only place, a narrow wooden bed.

We refused.

The carved box was nowhere to be seen. A machete such as was used to chop cane gleamed on the wall. A shotgun and a heavy ax leaned into a corner. Every settler had these. Nevertheless the atmosphere was portentous. He merely studied us and seemed to enjoy that, for now and then a faint smile moved his mustache. The thin dark pasted itself on the window.

When we could no longer see one another in the room, Old Loony took a lantern from the wall and lighted it. While he was raising the chimney and turning the wick up and down, he began to speak to us, or perhaps he was speaking to himself. I could make out very little of it, but finally this was clear: "Well, I promised and I must keep my promise." He hung the lantern back on the nail; its smoky light threw our long bending shadows across the floor and up the wall and gave his face a furtive look. "I did promise," he repeated.

He went to the bed and stooped with some care for his old joints and dragged out a small wooden box. It was not carved at all; it was of heavy rubbed wood and the top was curved like that of an old trunk. It had the charm of all miniatures and we gasped at once with delight; but then, with the shared thought of the hideous dried hand, we froze again into silence.

"Come here," he said, and we went.

He took a key from a gutstring around his neck and unlocked the little chest. We went down on our knees for a better view. He noticed this and smiled as if we were all in this terrible secret together.

When the curved lid was lifted, an odd fragrance rose, and in the dim light from the lantern dark swirls of polished hair shone and fell over the edges of the box. The old man slid his delicate fingers under the hair and lifted a part of it, which fell as if from a head. Our breath drew in against all will to prevent it.

"No need to be afraid. She's been dead long ago."

Something heavy and hard rattled around in the bottom of the box.

"Put it on," the old man urged and held the scalp with its long dark hair out to me. "You're older. It will suit you better. More like her."

When I hesitated, he placed it on my head and said, "Stand up!"

I was trembling. The hair fell to my fingertips. Permeating my fright was the scent of aromatic wood.

"Turn around."

I stood paralyzed as fear of the dead woman possessed me. The old man tipped his head to one side and smiled. "I pass the evenings sometimes brushing her hair. That's why it shines so."

Although I was only a girl, tall for my age and thin from hunger, he admired the beautiful hair once more adorning a living woman. He squinted his eyes to concentrate his vision; he did not smile, and he looked at me for a long time.

"Turn around," he commanded again, slowly, gently, almost in a whisper. "Walk, walk."

As I turned, as I walked, the long hair falling about me like a cape, he called out, his voice fierce and young. A woman's name. A cry. A wild lost sound. He shoved the box across the floor and leaped to his feet.

Marcy screamed. "Sister, look out! He's going to kill her again!"

I whirled to escape. He stopped, and his mouth, which had been hidden beneath his mustache, fell open pitifully. "You spoiled it," he said. His mouth closed, and the mustache trembled over it like a dried weed in a small wind. Then, shaking himself free of the dream, he shouted to Marcy, who was trying desperately to open the door. "Girl, don't do that!"

She stopped pulling at the latch and burst out crying.

"Don't do that!" he repeated and moved toward her. I stepped in his way, fiery with courage and fear.

He seemed bewildered. He gestured as if in appeal, but I thought that his eyes were wily and mad. Then he disregarded me and lifted the dead woman's hair from my head and placed it tenderly on the head of Marcy. "Here, you may try it on, too."

Marcy was sobbing now, and the dark hair placed askew on her own pale hair was but another horror. She took the rabbit's foot from her pocket and clutched it in plain view.

The old man went over to the little box and peered in it as if he had not seen it a thousand times before. He held up a brush for us to see, but still, when he touched the box, another object rattled hard against the wood. I tried to smile, to humor him. He sighed and picked up the box and carried it into the light of the lantern.

"Look here, children." He held out a horse's black hoof topped with a slender ankle of sorrel hair. "It was this did it."

We stared obligingly at the hoof, and then he put it back. "Burr was wild and skittish but she kept riding him. I didn't want her to, but she always said she had no use for a tame horse. Burr was naturally scared of snakes, all horses are, but he was deathly afraid of bobcats. I don't know why. One might've jumped on his back and sunk his claws in when Burr was a colt. You know, bobcats are rambling around in the rocks and brush day and night. Wellsir, a bobcat must have spooked him as they was picking their way down the side of a canyon. I'll say one thing, Burr never throwed her. She stayed on him. I heard them both screaming, woman and horse, when he lost his footing and fell all the way down the side to the bottom. I had to go down on foot. That canyon, little girls, was full of boulders and alive with rattlesnakes. I wouldn't have felt it if they had all bit me. But they didn't bother. When I got there, they was both done for. It was pitiful. I just sat there all that day and all that night. I don't mind telling you I cried like a woman. I heard animals in the night, so I lit my pipe. Sunup, I found a sharp rock, and it took me a long time but I made her a decent grave. Then, though I could hardly do it, I cut off her long hair. I had to have a keepsake. It's terrible hard when you have a person one day and the next day she is gone forever." He thought for a moment. "I picked wild flowers, not many in that place, and leaves, and made her a bed and covered her. I piled on a lot of rocks. After that I moved on, come here and settled. Took me all one winter to knot each hair into a piece of cloth." He sighed a long deep sigh. "I forget how old I am, but it's many a year, many a year."

We listened in awed silence to his story, and now he was silent. The night was silent, enclosing the hut like a great fur pocket. It was as if no one were in the room. When the stillness was taut to breaking, we heard a swift small running across the floor that ended on the old man's shoe. He said nothing, made no move, and the little banded gecko raced upward, holding on with his lizard feet that looked like hands, lifting his head as if for recognition. The old man turned and blinked.

We watched his small hand lift the gecko tenderly into his shirt pocket. His eyes still dazed with shadows, he looked at Marcy, unbelieving. The ridiculous sight of her slouched against the door, wiping her eyes, with the wig lopsided on her head, the dead hair hanging over her forlorn young face, must have broken a solemn and awful bond, for Old Loony began to laugh.

It was a low chuckle at first, a clumsy lurch of laughter that crashed, shattered like a flash flood through a dry streambed, clearing at last, sparkling, running pure. This laughter caught me and then Marcy, and we could not stop. We stumbled about, blind with tears, aching, helpless in release. While the old man was bent over, laughing, I snatched the long hair from my sister's head, flung it in the box, and closed the lid.

Seeing Marcy's tousled tomboy head once more, Old Loony's hilarity came to an end, but tears of laughter still ran gravely down his whiskered face.

He felt in his pocket for the frightened gecko, held him in his hand, and spoke to him. "He's my friend, stays with me winter and summer, hides all day and comes out at night to hunt spiders and insects and to keep me company. A fine little fellow." He dropped the gecko onto the bed, took the lantern from its nail, and offered to see us home. We thanked him, but there was no need. The stars were out, and if we watched them, we could find our way.

Outside the lantern ringed us in its solitary glow, the black night blacker beyond its rim. The wind had died down, the air was cold, but it was still a mild autumn night.

"I ought to see you little girls safe home."

"I'm not afraid of the night," I told him.

"Like an Indian," he said. "They was here, them and the buffalo, not too many years ago."

"Good night, sir," I said, having no name for him.

" 'Sir'! I'll be dad-blamed! 'Old Loony' is what they call me behind my back. I may just change it to 'Sir Loony.' Let's hear how it sounds."

"Good night, Sir Loony."

The old man laughed. "It's not half bad. Well, now, I declare. Sir Loony it is." He suddenly sniffed the air. "Smell that?" He was excited. "That sweet little drift of wind?"

We raised our heads and sniffed. "Snow."

"Spring! The very first whiff of spring, girls!"

"But . . ." Marcy began. I saw her hand take hold of the rabbit's foot.

"Girls, if you'll just notice, pert near every fall this little wind comes, or maybe a whole day of it, and it's a spring wind. It ain't fall. A hint. Me and my little gecko friend in there know we're going to get through another winter, then. Well, good night, little ladies. Come again."

I found the North Star. We hoisted our light sacks onto our backs and started. Away from the lantern our eyes grew accustomed to the star-polished dark. Stars were above and all around us, down to the black and circling land. We walked in a world of stars.

25

Once papa made a decision, he acted at once and expected us to do the same.

"Better study it over a bit," Grandfather advised.

"I know what I want to do, Dad. Besides, we've crowded you long enough."

"I never heard much about that before. I got used to it."

"We didn't."

"Well son, this is all the hospitality I have to offer."

Papa was ashamed. He dipped a stick into a can of axle grease and began greasing another wagon wheel. "We've got to get the girls to school. They're as wild as rabbits."

"I still know a few things they don't. I could teach them another winter."

"You only went to the third grade."

"In school," Grandfather said. "In life, I have read a good many books in my helter-skelter fashion, and so have you. I was brought up on the Bible, and although I have had my doubts, it

is a great book of life. Living out here in this wilderness, I've observed many things in nature that made me think twice. Only
the other morning it came to me clear as a bell that it was people
I doubted; I couldn't tolerate hypocrisy and cut-and-dried religion. I got all that mixed up with God, or whatever one is
pleased to call this mighty force in everything, everything! My
thoughts were little. It appears to me they're growing."

"Better than the crops," Papa said from the far side of the
wagon. He was quiet, hesitant, then: "This place rattles a few
inside locks all right. But I don't know. It's all a damn big mystery. I think about it sometimes. One thing I think: When you're
dead, you're dead."

I had my mouth open to tell about Daft when I remembered
my promise to Grandfather. He looked at me and said, nodding
toward Papa, "The time may come. . . . But no matter, he has
to live his own life. We all do."

"What are you going to do this winter, Dad, all alone?"

"Now I lived here alone for years and reckon I can do it again.
Have you noticed that some birds, some animals live together and
others are solitary?"

"Be sure to keep the barn clean. There's feed for the horses and
you've got a supply of groceries."

"I thank ye, sir."

"We'll be back in the spring. I'm thinking of that Clayton
place on the creek, ten miles over east, this side of Artesia. You
ought to move to Two Buttes when you prove up this land, and
court Mrs. Denny. She lives with a ghost. That's no way."

"She will have to look elsewhere," Grandfather said.

"She isn't looking."

"Well, then, I can go in there and enjoy a meal. I'll remind
you to let me handle my life."

Papa laughed.

"Hear that?" I asked.

"You have ears like a coyote," Papa said. "Or an Indian."

I lay on the ground listening and the beats came stronger,
hoofbeats. I stood up and could see no one on the road. The
horses must be below the plain on the road to the creek.

"Mama!" I called down into the dugout. "Someone's coming!"

"Who?"

"I won't tell. Come up."

By this time the two horses were in view, and just before they reached our gate, they began to race and we could hear Maxine laughing. Cooper opened the gate from his saddle and they rode in. Mama ran up the steps and stood in the yard, waiting. When Marcy came up, she stood behind Papa, who was wiping his hands clean, smiling and calling a welcome. Grandfather's eyes lighted.

Held safely in the saddle with him was their son, Elmo, a year old, wearing a pair of fringed chaps made by Maxine.

"The Cooper Lovelands calling!" Maxine shouted from the gate.

They dismounted. Cooper slapped the horses and they moved away.

"Good afternoon, Alonzo." They spoke together. "Hello, Babbs," Maxine said and ran to Mama, embracing her. "I'm pregnant again, Ginny!" She meant to whisper but the words came out for all to hear. She danced around, smiling at Cooper, who blushed.

"Cooper," Papa said, "you're going to have to get a surrey or a Ford to carry your family."

"No sir, Walt, we're going to ride horses, and we'll teach the kids to ride. Notice Elmo holding the saddle horn? Bo likes him."

"Sure did, Cooper. Say, your crop hailed out, too?"

"No hail our way, so I can let you have seed so long as we're all raising row crops. Starting a herd of Herefords, going to build it up. I want to make enough money to buy a truck. We dug our well. Maxine's going to plant a garden come spring."

"Say! Cooper, you're doing all right."

"Well, proving up the land helps, and I can use the range. Nobody near us. We're making do with a mighty little house and mighty little money, but we're aiming for a ranch someday. Tullery said he hates to see you folks leave here. You for sure coming back to plant?"

"Can't give up now."

"Alonzo," Maxine said, "you've got to spend Thanksgiving and Christmas with us if the Whiteheads haven't got you ahead of us. And you're welcome anytime. Well, will you give us a promise, sir?"

"I'm not much for going visiting," Grandfather said, "but seeing it's you and Cooper, I'll say yes."

"Oh, goody!"

Mama looked glad, and I was so happy I nearly cried. Grandfather and I were going to write letters, but I knew how seldom he went to town for mail. He had told me he knew better how to get along alone than we did and that I was not to worry.

"Carrie and Jim are going to stop in when they go to town and see if he needs any supplies," Mama said. "I just love you and Carrie and I'm going to miss you both even if we haven't had a chance to visit much."

"Goddang my wildcats!" Grandfather said, suddenly angry. "All of you worrying as if I'm old and stiff and helpless! I can take care of my own needs, dang it!"

"Forevermore!" Maxine said. "Grandfather Alonzo Babb! I do admire your spunk. But we all need one another. What would I do without Cooper?"

Grandfather could not simmer down at once, but he made a wordless apologetic sound. Maxine stepped closer to him and said seriously, "Alonzo—you see, if you were so old, I wouldn't dare call you by your first name—Alonzo, the reason we want you to come over is to start being Elmo's grandpa. Cooper hasn't any folks. Kids like grandparents for some reason."

Grandfather glanced down at me and rapped my shoulder with his dark bony knuckles. "Yes, indeed. It works both ways." Grandfather's fierce black eyes were gentle again when he nodded at Maxine. He was not a man for smiling, and she knew what his nod meant.

"Nobody visits poor old Sir Loony," I said.

"Well," said Grandfather, "I draw the line there."

I was disappointed, but if they had lived there all those years and felt no need to get acquainted, their ways were beyond my young understanding.

"A couple of hermits," Papa said. "Both of them tough as boots. They'll be all right."

Grandfather looked pleased, then smiled, and we all watched him smile. His teeth came out from under his black mustache. "Well, have you all had your say?" He laughed, just a small laugh. It appeared that he was laughing at everyone, without meanness, with patience and affection.

26

WITH A RENTER IN VIEW, the elderly Claytons wanted to move to town before winter. Rather than risk losing the farm, Papa agreed at once. They offered a fair crop agreement as rent and sold us their chickens and a flock of guinea fowl. Papa had already bought their pigs. We had to give up our plans for moving to Elkhart and going to school.

While the men made their annual trip to the cedars for firewood for Grandfather, Mama worked at restoring the dugout to its bachelor state. The piano was to remain until spring when someone in town might buy and restore it, since we couldn't afford the repairs ourselves. With the added doghouse entrance, getting the piano out would be far more difficult than bringing it in. We had few possessions to move: the large brass bed and bedding, our clothes and small personal belongings.

"If you get too lonesome, Dad," Papa said on our last evening at Grandfather's, "you can move over to the Clayton place with

us." Mama whispered to me, "There they go again." But Grandfather said, "No. I'll drive over to visit. Better let well enough
alone."

Grandfather was a man who could live without the company
of other men and remain intact. He was not embarrassed to claim
creatures as his friends. A few friends among men were all he
needed, or could handle, and they were far removed in the past.

"Man is the only one out of kilter," he said to Papa. "And
the chances are he has it in him to get back when he finds out
he's a part of nature and not its lord and master. Right here,
now, if we plow up all this grassland and kill off all the wild
animals, there'll be a hard price to pay."

"God's wrath, you mean?" Papa said, testing him.

"Cause and effect, I call it. Mayhap part of a design we're too
weak-minded to understand yet."

"Is that all?"

"That's a good deal, son. But I'm thinking there's more."

"Well, my Grandmother Walker always said you'd come around
to her beliefs."

"I haven't, haven't at all. Her beliefs were all right for her,
strict, full of a world of man-made rules and dogma. The same
with my own folks. That suited them. I'm exploring, you may
call it, without those rules."

"Anyway, she said she'd pray for you even if you had killed
her daughter, my own mother."

"Strong language," Grandfather said with distaste.

"She said you were off on a wild jaunt."

"I was striking out on my own, farther west, so we could get
away from all the dang relations, all the dang Welsh and Irish
talking about the old country."

"They were good people," Papa said. "If they hadn't fed sister
and me while you were drunk, we'd have starved. But you didn't
care."

At this, Grandfather clucked his tongue. "I was on my way back
with a job. The baby came early and the doctor did his best. I
never had a drink until your mother died like that, sudden and
me away. I loved your mother."

They went through this quarrel about once a year as if it were
a ritual they were required to perform, with the lines perfectly
known and the aftermath painful for days. At the end of the

quarrel, Papa made comments about Grandfather, words we knew by heart, as if he were not in the room. "He was a dreamer, couldn't make his dreams work. Another thing, they eloped, and that went against the grain of my mother's folks. They were strait-laced. There's a lot you girls don't know about Alonzo."

"Let it lie," Grandfather said. "I'm Lucifer."

Papa ignored him and kept on. With each detail, his anger dissipated, his tone changed. "When Dad straightened up, I was a young boy, and he used to take me to early Socialist meetings of farmers, and we read the Socialist newspaper. I learned a lot about both sides of the fence. But I wouldn't join anything; I'd heard all those people from the old country praising this country. I liked being a free man, still do. I wouldn't join anything; I've got my own ideas."

"As I have my own," Grandfather said from his position of banishment. "I would like to see every living thing—plant and animal—have a fair chance at life. But politics isn't—well, politics means power, and, as I read once, power corrupts."

"He was always reading Thomas Paine, then Ingersoll. Then he got to drawing pictures." He finally spoke to Grandfather. "What became of all those different ideas you had?"

"If you don't mind, son, I'll keep my distance."

"What is this you believe now? Tell us some more."

At this, Grandfather, whose best thoughts had been interrupted earlier, and who had been sitting rather dejectedly on his cot in an effort to appear absent, sat up straight, his hooded eyes opening wider, black and indignant.

"Can't a man have his own thoughts?"

"Yes, sir, he can." Papa spoke with respect.

Pleased, surprised even, Grandfather said, "I will just say a man's mind keeps opening when he lets it."

27

THE GATE TO the Clayton place, two tall upright posts with a long post on top, led simply into more of the plain without a house or any sign of habitation in sight. Papa said nothing. We passed a field of cane stubble fenced at one end of the large gray pasture and drove on and on until we came to the very edge of a precipice, apparently a continuation of the one from which Daft had leaped to his death. Below we saw cottonwood and willow trees along one side of a shallow creek with a wide sandy shore, a beautiful scene. Tears came to Mama's eyes.

Papa smiled. "You see what the head of the house found! Now, hang on for dear life!"

He tightened the reins and pulled the wagon brake, and we started down a treacherous, rocky, almost vertical road. The big mares went stiff-legged, braking themselves; the wagon rolled against their rumps. We were frightened but it was too late to get out and walk down. The road curved, bringing us into the farmyard, a long narrow shelf of rocky land, running east and west, its southern edge a lesser precipice above the creek. A one-room stone house with a pen attached housed two pigs. At the far end of this ledge was a barn, its boards weathered gray. A path led to the barn. The wagon must remain near the road where the ledge was wider. The history of this farm was revealed in what must have been its first home, a dugout, now occupied by chickens.

Near the creek bluff, midway between house and barn, was a well with a hand pump. Below to the south stretched the scene of sandy shore and trees. Beyond the barn, where the ledge ended, the creek traveled at the foot of a very high rock wall, its upper portion covered with the mud nests of swallows. Scattered along the stream were huge stones rounded and smoothed by thousands of years of weather.

It was an odd place, and the house we were to live in the oddest of all. It was simple, two rooms, a flat roof, but it was perched on a tiny rock mesa with steep shale sides and a narrow collar of the same rocky earth around it. One would slide rather than walk down the two paths. The precipice wall that backed the house and barn, and continued along the creek, broke midway into a wild canyon choked with gigantic rocks and heavy brush. The canyon opened into the farmyard, and on its far side was a perfect rock-walled, roofless room, a natural formation, with a red berry tree at its corner entrance. It was like a dreamed place. Along the path to the barn, on the creek side, was a narrow strip of alfalfa where later we turned the horses and pigs loose, but not at the same time. Everything was in a row on the ledge. The high drop from the plain appeared to be crowding the farm buildings toward the embankment; the savage canyon suggested danger, but the trees and the peaceful, wide creekbed with its slender glistening stream provided the main view from the house.

We sat in the wagon looking at this harsh and beautiful place so imaginatively wind-shaped and water-carved, burned by the sun, cooled by the clear stream. Leaves still on the cottonwoods flashed in the pure light. There was an airy serenity quite unlike the primal stillness of the plain. We listened to the small harmonies of running water and leaves in wind and the quiet autumn conversation of birds. We saw at once that there were more birds here than on the arid grassland; that very evening we were to hear a mockingbird singing for hours from a high place.

"Oh, Walt!" Mama said and leaned against him in thanks. "Water and trees!"

"The house isn't so good," he said.

"We won't mind."

Marcy and I could hardly wait to visit the rock room and to explore our way down the sheer eroded bank into the creek.

"Better unload," Papa said, "and we'll get busy. I've got to make a bunk for the girls from some of that old lumber piled there by the grindstone. I'll give it a good washing first and dry it out. They can sleep on the floor a few nights."

The Claytons had already left in order to reach their town home before dark. The house was clean, dusty only where furniture had been removed. A wood-burning stove and an old table and chairs were in the kitchen. The other room was empty save for a stand with two books on it. Books! A change from *Kit Carson* and the *Denver Post*. One was on agriculture, one a large collection of old tales and narrative poems. I opened this book at random and read aloud these lines:

> Maud Muller on a summer's day
> Raked the meadow sweet with hay. . . .

"Look at this!" Mama called from the kitchen. "Well, I'll declare!" She had lifted a clean cloth from a large chipped plate. There in the center were twelve hard-boiled eggs in their shells, still warm. Each egg had been barely cracked to admit air and allow the shell to come easily away from the glossy white.

We were hungry. It seemed that we had been hungry ever since we came to Colorado. The four of us washed our hands in a granite pan. Water, all we needed! Water! Books! Food! We stood about, eating the eggs, praising the Claytons.

"I'll water and feed the horses now and let them rest," Papa said. "I'll feed the chickens today, and after this, you girls will feed them and pump fresh water for them every day. Then I'll show you how to clean the henhouse."

"I want to help clean the house," Marcy said. "I want to shine the windows."

"Good!" Mama said, who did not care for housework any more than I but did it from a sense of order.

"The only thing wrong is that we cannot look out these windows and see the bugs walking around." Marcy was disappointed, and stood with her head down. Suddenly she yelped and leaped toward Papa. A large hairy tarantula on the windowsill appeared to be looking at her from all eight eyes. A night hunter by touch, and a ground dweller, it should not have been in the house by day, but there it was, not even running away, a ferocious-looking creature.

"Will it bite?" Marcy wanted to know.

"Sure, it'll bite, and it might be poisonous; some are, some not. Take no chances." As the spider did not move, Papa said, "Now, I'll show you something. They can't see well. Watch, but keep clear. They can jump." He whistled a song, disturbing the air near the tarantula. "Pretty sure she's a female." She moved slightly. Then he waved a stick in front of her and she backed. Suddenly, threatened, she stood up on her hind legs, four of the eight, and her jaws moved once up and down. An almost inaudible soft purr came from her. We drew back, but remained close enough to see the lovely iridescent hairs on the pads of her feet. Her body was brownish black, the leg joints nearest the body brown, the rest tan.

"All right, old lady," Papa said. "Just wanted you to show your spunk. You know, girls, she probably came in to eat the book mites."

Mama brought a glass jar and handed it to him. "Hurry! That hairy thing scares the daylights out of me."

Papa nudged the tarantula into the jar. "I'll let her loose in the canyon. She won't come back."

"Never in her life and after, I hope." Mama shuddered.

"Well, if it's a female, she may live fifteen or twenty years. If it's a male, he'll be gone in a year or two."

"How do you know?" I asked.

"When I was a boy, a fellow had one for a pet. He said she was seventeen years old, then. He caught us boys teasing her once, got her riled up, and he wouldn't let us watch her anymore."

Papa went into the canyon a ways and opened the jar; he tipped it, and the tarantula slid out and ran for cover. On the ground she was hard to see and I reminded my bare feet to "look out."

"Didn't even say thank you, kiss my foot, or anything, just ran,"

Papa said, laughing. He stopped laughing and listened. "Hear that?"

"Yes, rattlesnakes rattling."

We ran back to the path.

"You girls stay out of this canyon. Clayton said it's alive with rattlers. He killed a hundred and twenty-two this summer here and up in the field."

I went in to tell that scary news.

"Good grief!" Mama said. "This country still belongs to its animals."

For these and many other creatures we had encountered, fear was seldom in our minds; they lived here, too, and we were to take care.

Papa was shouting at us. We hurried out onto the narrow collar around the house.

"Look at the water!" A shining stream was pouring from the iron mouth as he pumped. "No more hauling water and wrestling with those barrels! Isn't this a pretty sight! We'll have to get Dad over here when he proves up his claim."

"Mercy!" Mama said under her breath. "He can have the dugout." She giggled.

I did not understand.

"It would not be so bad if we had more room, Chey. That's all I meant."

I put my arm around her; I loved her even more than I loved Grandfather, but I did not really understand how much harder our life was for her than for Marcy and me, and how quietly courageous she was.

28

If it had not been that the plain resumed its flat and open expanse beyond the creek, we should have felt shut in. Our eyes were accustomed to distance, our minds to the freedom of space, our very beings to the inscrutable power of earth and sky seemingly endless and unmolested. We knew this before in our separate ways, but we knew it more deeply when a high rock wall cut the circle in two. Aside from the scattered cottonwoods and the fallen white trunks of dead trees, nothing obstructed our view to the south. The sandy shore ended in a low eroded bank; the plain began again and went its way to the far horizon.

"We ought to go someplace for a change until we get used to it," Papa said one morning when we were well settled into the house, and familiar with our new chores. "It'll soon be winter. Artesia is five miles east, where your mother will get her mail." Papa winked at us.

Mama began to change her clothes. "Some letters may be there already!" She handed Marcy and me freshly ironed dresses and our old sweaters, clean and much mended. Papa put on clean overalls and shirt.

"We'll walk," he said. "Get the feel of open land again."

"I wouldn't miss it for anything," Mama said dryly.

"Your mother doesn't care for the plains," Papa said to us, as if we didn't know it.

"Ready!" Mama was animated and pretty.

"We'll get acquainted with the storekeeper and buy a few supplies that we can carry. When we can afford it, we'll take the wagon and get more."

"Listen." We stepped outside. The sounds came steadily on and abruptly became loud and violent. In a few minutes Grandfather's wagon lurched and tipped dangerously down the steep road, his horses galloping out of control. Grandfather was leaning far back, braced against the seat, pulling tight reins.

"It's a runaway!" Papa shouted. He slipped and slid down into the yard and ran toward the horses, reaching for their bridles again and again before he caught hold. Their mad speed swung him off his feet but he was strong, regaining his stride, running with them, speaking softly in an effort to calm them. They ran through the yard toward the barn, where there was no road for the wagon. If they turned aside, they and the wagon and Grandfather would go over the fifteen-foot bluff and into the creek. Whether Papa's words or their ending hysteria steadied them, they stopped at the well and stood trembling, their great bellies heaving with breath. Grandfather leaped to the ground.

"A rattlesnake spooked them. Plague on that road of yours!" Grandfather looked excited and young, as if he had enjoyed the danger.

Little Bugs, excited too, was like a new horse, the way he was meant to be. I was glad to see him and Dip. When they were rested, they walked slowly to the water tank and drank.

"I'll unhitch them and let them graze, Dad. We're walking to Artesia. Going for a lark."

"I've just had one."

"Come on, Dad!"

"By Jove, let a man catch his breath and have a drink."

Papa filled the dipper hanging on the pump and handed Grandfather a drink of our good water. "You hungry?"

"No more than usual. I'll do."

"I'm bringing some hard-boiled eggs," Mama said, as we started up the steep road.

Papa and Grandfather were leading the horses by rope halters, which they removed and threw on the ground when we reached the top. The horses were a little skittish at first but they moved off and began to crop grass. Katy and Buff were near the gate, a long walk, and as we passed, they lifted their heads and watched us for a time.

Out on the road, Mama and Papa and Marcy went ahead; Grandfather and I dropped back. The wind was blowing and great tumbleweeds rolled over the plain, scattering their seeds and piling up against the only fence in sight. Some of them were five and six feet across, full of stickers, their single roots as small as pig tails, to be easily wrenched free by the autumn winds. There was spring wind, summer wind, autumn wind, and winter wind.

"Grandfather, have you seen Fred?"

Grandfather clucked his tongue.

"*Have* you?" I said.

"No, I have not. I have not had time to see Daft either. I am getting ready for the winter."

"Are you mad at me for asking?"

"Not at all, child." We walked a long way in silence. "Isn't it better for you to take an interest in other things?"

"Aren't they all the same?"

"You've confounded me there."

"Well, I am interested in everything!"

He smiled. "In that case, I may say I have reason to believe Dip and Bugs saw him in the barn. Bugs had a conniption fit and would not go in his stall. Dip was excited, seemed glad, and whinnied. That stall was below zero, then it was warm, and the horses calmed down."

"I would like to see Fred."

"Fred was a workhorse, worked hard all his life. It may be he's taking a good rest."

"Does the spirit or the pure self get tired?"

"I can't answer that, but I wouldn't be surprised."

When we came to Artesia, there was only one small building, its shed, and an outhouse. The post office was in one corner of the store, a cubicle with a general delivery window. Mr. Starbuck was the storekeeper and postmaster, but Mrs. Starbuck was putting up the mail.

A farmer with a big stack of supplies on the counter was paying for them with silver dollars.

"Hear you had a good crop of broomcorn this year, Clyde?"

"Sure did. First crop in four years. Near starved out. Starbuck, I don't know what we'd a done without credit. Oughta give you storekeepers a medal. I'm right proud to pay up today."

"Glad you can, Clyde. I'll be lookin' for that medal."

"Reckon your Missus will pick me out a pretty piece of gingham? Wife's birthday."

The Starbucks had greeted us and left us alone while we looked around.

Now Mrs. Starbuck went to a shelf and took down a bolt of cloth. "She was wishin' on this one day. It's twenty cents, five yards will be aplenty for a dress."

He gave her a dollar. When she had wrapped the cloth, she hurried back to the post office. Papa introduced himself and us to Mr. Starbuck, and the storekeeper introduced Clyde Sykes, who was carrying out his supplies.

"Hold on a minute, Clyde," said Mrs. Starbuck. "Listen to this, Ben, and you folks, too, if you know him. Here's a card from Tuck Coleman to his sister, Ella. Says he's talked on a telephone and knows she sure would enjoy having one. Ha. Says the war is getting worse. . . ."

"What war is that?" Clyde Sykes asked. "If it isn't one, it's another. Foreigners always fighting."

"Now wait! Says there's talk at the plant we'll get into it. If we do, says he'll join up so's he can meet a French mam'selle." Mrs. Starbuck stopped reading. "That dumb brute, more likely he'll get killed or lose a leg and arm."

"Only good thing a war would do for us is to raise the price of broomcorn," Sykes said. "And that'd sure as hell be bloody money, I don't care what you say."

"That's the truth," Papa said.

The three men began to talk about the times.

Mrs. Starbuck said to Mama, "Tuck went back East over a year ago, works for Ford Motor Company, gets *five* dollars a day! That boy must have all kinds of money by now. Didn't like to farm or ranch. He's getting citified. . . . French mam'selle, indeed!"

Mama smiled. She was no gossip. In town, people used to bring her their troubles, sure of her ear and sympathy.

"I wonder if any mail has come for us, forwarded from Two Buttes? I wrote everyone to write me here."

"Artesia. Population five." Mrs. Starbuck laughed. "We have three half-grown children, two boys and a girl, a big help." She looked through the new mail much faster now, and shoved five letters under the window grill. "I'll swan, if you don't get more mail than anyone around here! Liven us up!"

"Oh, thank you!"

"Got any secrets, tell your folks not to write cards. I read the cards, keeps me from getting lonesome, I guess. Nothing private about a card, anyway. But you'd be surprised what some people will write out in the open."

Grandfather bought a bottle of liniment and an eighth of a pound of camphor, and Papa bought some rough nails.

"I've a mind to buy some cheese and crackers," Grandfather said, and made up his mind slowly.

Mr. Starbuck uncovered the big yellow wheel of cheese, bore down on the knife, separating a mouth-watering wedge. He looked up at Marcy and me, then cut two thin pieces for us to eat right there. Mr. Starbuck made a very good impression on us and received our glad thanks. Mrs. Starbuck came out of her cubicle again and reached into a slanting glass jar and handed us each a cookie.

"Ben, children would rather have gingersnaps anyday." She handed one to Mama and offered a treat to the men. They refused proudly though I knew they were hungry.

On the way home, the men walked and talked together. Once I heard Papa say, "The damn world. Those fellows up in Washington ought to come out on the earth and take a breath of fresh air and look around once in awhile. Damn world, anyway."

Again I had a sensation of going to the horizon, lifting up the sky, and walking out into the world.

29

One chilly autumn day the Claytons came for a visit. For a change, the chickens were not scattered all over the ledge but were scratching around their dugout, several of them dusting their feathers in the ash pile. The Claytons drove expertly down the steep road and stopped their spring wagon before frightening the lordly rooster, Brigham (after Brigham Young), and his flock. The elderly couple walked slowly toward the chickens and stood watching them. Papa was stacking fodder he had gathered in the field the day before. It was a volunteer crop that had come up in the spring without help from Mr. Clayton, as he had not farmed last season. Mama came from the house. Papa quit his work, and we all went to welcome the Claytons.

"By doggy, I'm ashamed to tell you folks why we came," Mr. Clayton said. "Wife and I miss the farm, and we miss these chickens something terrible."

Mama said sympathetically, "I expect you do."

Papa looked disappointed, but he said, "You wouldn't want to move back here with winter coming on, would you?"

"We've stood many a winter here, young man. Bones feel the cold more now, it's a fact, but wife and—"

"It's him," Mrs. Clayton said. "In town he has nothing to do with his time. It wearies him."

"I say I'd rather wear out than rust out," he said.

"My work is about the same except for—"

Mr. Clayton interrupted her. "What would you say, Babb, to us buying the chickens back? I'd have a little something to do. House there has a good henhouse and fenced yard."

"I told him we ought to buy some new chickens and not bother you folks, but he likes these old fowl."

"Well, got them all named just about, as I told you. They know me, and that's more than I can say for the people in town."

Papa was so relieved not to lose the farm, although he liked the chickens too, that he said at once, "You take them. They're yours anyway. I'll buy some baby chicks in the spring. I like to raise them."

Mr. Clayton objected.

Papa said, "No, that's no more than right."

"Tell you what I'll do, Babb. Spring, I'll bring you a couple or three hens and as many setting eggs as they can cover. You'll soon have a flock and eggs."

"Well, I thank you, sir."

"Would you like to come in and have some alfalfa tea?" Mama asked. She had been drying stems and leaves. Carrie had suggested it.

"I would, indeed," Mrs. Clayton said, "but I'd better help this old coot of mine catch these chickens, and then we'd better get for home."

Mr. Clayton took a handful of corn from his pocket and threw it at his feet. Brigham, suspicious, stood apart. The hens, after a few pecks down the favored line, gathered to eat. Mr. Clayton called them by name; he had his favorites as did the rooster, and they answered him. "By doggy!" he said in a low, pleased voice. Papa had gone to his wagon and brought back the coops. Mr. Clayton sprinkled corn into the wire coops and the hens went in. Papa was forced to chase Brigham, a good runner, for some time before he succeeded in catching him against the cliff.

When the Claytons were ready, Mama brought them a jar of dried alfalfa to take home. The loss of the hens with their busy lives, their clucking, cackling, murmuring, and the rooster's crowing, made the farm suddenly empty.

"That's bad luck," Papa said, adding, "Damn superstition, but it's bad luck." He went to the barn to work and to turn the horses loose. We heard him quarreling with Katy. In another moment we saw him flying out the barn door as if running backwards in the air. He landed on his back and leaped up immediately. We laughed, then fearing he might be hurt, we ran down the long path to him. He looked sheepish as he limped toward the house, passing us.

"Oh, Walt, are you hurt, honey?"

"Leave me alone, damn it. I'm all right."

We turned back, following him.

"What on earth happened?"

"Damn mare started to kick me."

"What did you do to Katy?" I asked.

"You keep out of this! She nipped at me and I hit her with my fist."

"Poor Katy!"

"Poor Katy, hell! She's got it in for me."

"All you have to do is treat her with respect. Grandfather said so."

Papa laughed. "Well, I reckon I'll have to. I'll say one thing for her. She held her strength. She could have killed me. Knocked me off balance and I got out of the way fast."

"We noticed that," Mama said.

Papa quit limping and turned back. "I'm going to finish that fodder job." He saw Marcy's scared face. "What's the matter, pard, you think your dad was hurt? Not me!"

"Do you want my rabbit's foot?" she asked.

"I may need it next time I go in the barn. But you keep it now."

She followed him, then hippety-hopped alongside, holding his hand.

"I wonder what we're going to eat this winter?" Mama said as we walked back past the canyon to the house. "No eggs, and no chickens in a pinch. Our harvest money gone before we've got anything like a winter supply. Your dad keeps saying once we get a foothold here, we'll be all right."

"Won't we?"

"I just don't know, but we'll try."

30

PAPA WORKED WITH Jim Whitehead, trading his labor for grain to add to our winter supply for the horses. He and Grandfather had saved less than a ton of broomcorn after the hail. The storm had missed Jim's fields and he had marketed some of his steers. Carrie had canned vegetables from her garden. We made a small barrel of hominy from corn, intending to put it up in jars for the winter, but it fermented and exploded.

"Jim and Cooper have the right idea about surviving in this country," Papa said. "They're building up herds. Someday, with water, this will be rich farmland, but people like us have to come in here first to prove you can starve to death on dry land. That's our purpose." He was bitter. Then gazing out over the plain and at the big sky, he said, "Yet where else can a man see so far?"

Once again we listened to the Canadian geese flying south, saw the cottonwood leaves waver down like little kites, heard the quieting natural sounds, felt the slowing of wilderness in preparation for rest. Coyotes lapping water from the creek appeared larger in their winter fur. The horses' coats grew heavier. When Grandfather came to visit, he wore his greatcoat that came nearly to his ankles. Bounce was bushy with thickening hair. Only we were ill-provided for the season, or so it seemed; and not for lack of foresight.

When the first winter winds blew from the northwest, down from the distant Rocky Mountains, the high cliff wall sheltered our house and barn on the ledge. There was feed for the two pigs and the horses, and the guineas when they deigned to come home. They roamed in a flock over the plain, gave their alarms, and "hid out," as they would hide their nests in the spring. They belonged only to themselves. We had driftwood and cow chips to burn and a thick Sears, Roebuck catalog to look at when we were not reading from the two books left by the Claytons. Marcy amused herself for long hours at a time cutting furniture from the catalog, arranging it in dream-house rooms whose walls were the two books and cardboard from last year's Christmas boxes.

Christmas came with icy winds, and the New Year with snow so deep only those who must tend their stock on the range ventured out. As soon as we could, we dressed in our warmest clothes, wrapped ourselves in heavy quilts, and drove to see Grandfather. He was glad to see us, but his pride was hurt that we should doubt his ability to look after himself. We did not doubt it, but our presence showed concern. Nevertheless, he and Papa drove to the creek for water, taking an ax along to break the ice. While the men were gone, we cleaned the dugout of its bachelor neglect, and Mama lovingly dusted her red mahogany piano, even raising the lid and rippling a finger along the silent keys. She made corn bread in a skillet on the little monkey stove and its fragrance greeted the men on their return. Bounce yipped in pleasure at this change of fare and ate his piece as hungrily as we.

"I ought to give you girls a spelling lesson. I've been making a long list," Grandfather said.

Papa went to clean the barn. When he came back, we had finished spelling, and Grandfather gave us, in his spidery handwriting, a list of new words and their meanings to learn at home.

"That barn hasn't been cleaned for three or four days!" Papa said.

"Because of the blizzard."

"Blizzard, the devil!"

Grandfather turned back to Marcy and me. "You see, girls, how easy it is to put your head in a hornet's nest."

"You could rake or shovel that horse dung out every day in a few minutes."

"I see to it in my way."

"Some way!"

"Ain't nature grand," Mama said, quoting a daily cartoon called "Fay and Stell" in the *Denver Post.* "Human nature, I mean."

Papa snorted.

"Believe it or not, Alonzo," Mama said, "we came to wish you a Happy New Year."

"I thank ye. You've cleaned everything up just dandy." He glanced at Papa. "Even the barn."

Papa, glad to be helped out of his temper, smiled and said, "Say, Dad, that little Bugs is all right, never carries his head down anymore."

Grandfather brought from behind the stove two small boxes he had made for Marcy and me. The wood was rubbed and the lids had tiny brass hinges and latches and pins. "For your keepsakes." We were delighted. I did think briefly of Old Loony's keepsake box filled with his dead wife's hair.

"It goes without saying I didn't visit the Cooper Lovelands Christmas Day. But danged if Maxine didn't send Cooper over on his horse to bring me a gallon bucketful of good stew and a loaf of homemade bread."

After we had heard the news of the Lovelands, Papa said we should start back before dark. Grandfather put on his long coat and stood outside with Bounce at his side and watched us drive away.

"You didn't tell him how low we are on food, did you?" Papa asked Mama.

"I didn't even mention food."

"You girls didn't say anything?"

"We know we aren't supposed to," Marcy said.

"That's right. Never go around telling your troubles. Keep your dignity. That's about all we've got right now, girls, but things won't stay like this. Another thing, you go around singing the blues all the time and people don't like you. They may even give you another kick."

"Not all," Mama said.

"No, not all, but damn few won't."

"I like to listen to people's troubles. And it kinda helps just to tell them."

"Well, so do I. I listen. But if a man never has anything else to talk about, I'll see him coming before he sees me."

"Poor soul."

"Not poor soul. If he never tells me any of his good news, something's wrong. It isn't all bad. Look at us."

"Just the same," Mama said, "I think I will write to Mom."

"No you don't. We'll make it all right."

"But—oh, it's getting too cold to talk. This wind feels like a knife in my lungs and my teeth are freezing."

When we got home in the dark, the house was so cold we went right to bed. Papa threw a few ears of corn to Hannah and Prince Pig, who had gone into their snug stone house and were asleep on the hay in the corner. He unharnessed the mares and led them by the water trough, where he had to break the ice. In the barn, he fed them and hurried back to the house and into bed. We were all tired and sleepy, and anyway, when we were hungry, it was better to go to sleep.

31

IN THE EARLY SPRING before the earth was warm enough for seeds, before the leaf buds on the cottonwoods unfurled, while the little junco snowbirds still sang their winter songs, a time came when we had nothing to eat for seven days. Mama had scrimped all winter, stretched our few supplies of pinto beans, flour and corn and lard until the day they vanished completely. All we had left was salt and red and black pepper. From these we made "pepper tea," which was hot water with a sprinkling of pepper to deceive the taste buds, a last-resort recipe for the "starved out." We grew very weak, not alone from the seven days fasting but from the long periods over the years when we had less than we needed, and almost none of the fresh vegetables and fruits we craved. We cared for the animals, who were now on short rations, did the necessary work of house and farm, and slept a great deal. It was a way to forget hunger.

"But," Papa said, "we have to keep moving, too. We don't want to lay around so much we can't get up."

One morning even he overslept. Mama whispered to Marcy and me to go with her to the well for water. It was hard for us to climb down and up the steep sides of the small rocky mesa upon which our house was perched. We were shaky and light-headed. I felt very tall and fluffy and it seemed to me I was taking great steps above ground, walking on air. In a way it was lovely. Every sight and sound was delicately intensified. At any moment I should fly or float into the crisp morning air and find myself across the creek, drifting on and on. This treacherous euphoria followed days of intense hunger, stomach cramps, and headache.

Mama leaned her weight upon the pump handle and moved it up and down with great effort until the water rose and filled our pail. Then she simply sat on the ground without meaning to, her face wet with perspiration, her breathing long exhausted sighs. She began to tremble.

"I'm all right," she said, seeing our fright. "Now listen. Do you girls feel strong enough to get down the bank and back?"

We nodded yes without thinking of no.

"Take this other bucket. If there are any minnows swimming in the creek, make a little dam and get them to swim into this. I'll stay here and watch. If you can't get back up, we'll wake your dad."

Her request excited our energy. There was no problem getting down the bank; we slid down. The stream was only a few inches deep and five or six feet across. We found a narrow place and built a dam of pebbles and sand. No minnows came. While we were engaged in repairing our dam, one minnow slipped past; then a small school flashed in the clear water, turned away from the dam to find an opening, and swam into our bucket. We counted nine and called the number up to Mama.

"Poor little things!" Marcy and I said to them as they flapped about in the shallow water of their prison. Nevertheless we watched for more and caught three. No more came. "They know and are hiding under rocks, and I don't blame them," Marcy said.

We searched for a place in the eroded bank where we could climb and catch hold of roots. When we finally reached the top, panting and quivery, Mama said, "Good girls!" We lay down to rest before climbing to the house. On the way Mama picked up a handful of pebbles. "I'll drop them in our fish soup. Maybe they'll add something."

We woke Papa and gave him a bowl of hot water and cayenne pepper with five minnows. "For the big bear," Mama said.

He looked into the bowl and smiled. "Well, I'll be damned, girls." When he had finished eating, he said, "I've got one shell left and I'd better save it for a rabbit. We've got to get strength enough to climb up that cliff and plant a garden this spring." Except for the narrow strip of alfalfa, there was no planting soil on our ledge. Both garden and field were up on the plain.

"This will last us a day or two," Mama said.

Russian thistles began to come up on the plain. Marcy and I gathered them, but we were still very hungry. The day that Papa took the gun and crossed the creek, we were afraid. When he left he said, "If any cattle are on the plain, I'm desperate enough to kill a calf."

"Oh, don't!" Mama pleaded with him. "You'll get in trouble! And don't go far, you're weak."

While he was gone, Jim Whitehead came down the road on horseback, left his horse by the water tank, and came to the house. When we visited back and forth, we were all in the habit of taking a small gift of homemade food or some useful thing we had made. Our gifts were usually crocheted or tatted lace from thread sent by Mama's mother. We could hardly wait to see what Jim had brought, hoping for a jar of food from Carrie's cellar shelf.

Jim wanted to visit with Papa and sat down to wait.

"Oh, yes, brought you something," he said and took from his pocket a jar of tomato preserves. "Taste good with all kinds of food, I think." Then he gave Mama six or eight little folds of catalog sheets, each labeled. "Seeds for your garden. The Claytons had one up above the barn. Better have Walt check the fence up there. Carrie fixed up these seeds for you before she left."

"Left?"

"Wouldn't even let me drive her to Lamar to the train this time. Got Doc Burtis to drive her from Two Buttes. Gone to her mother's, mad as a wet hen." He sat looking down at his hands. A vein swelled and throbbed along the side of his forehead.

"She'll be back in time to plant the garden," Mama said gently.

"I figured that, but I don't know. Said she wasn't coming back. Sure lonesome without her and Dale."

"I know she'll come back."

He looked up, his face eager, then guarded. "How do you know? Did she write you?"

"No. But I know how she feels. She—"

"I know, I've got to watch this damn temper. Say a lot of things I don't mean and then have to pay for it."

Papa came in the door with a big jackrabbit. We could hardly believe our good fortune. Papa was no hunter and, besides, there was little to hunt after the ruthless killing of the buffalo and the prairie chickens. That poor jackrabbit looked as big as a buffalo. Papa stood his gun in the corner of the kitchen. The two men greeted each other and Jim repeated his bad news.

"The thing for you to do, Jim, is wait a week, let her have a good visit, then just go after her and act like nothing ever happened."

"Is that what you'd do, Walt?" Jim had a crooked smile on his face and he winked at Mama.

"No, don't suppose I would. Ginny left me once and I wrote her a lot of letters to come back. I was in the wrong, and so are you, Jim."

"Walt forgot all about his pride then." Mama was already at the cook table preparing the rabbit. "Stay for dinner, Jim."

"Sure, Jim, stay. Do us all good. I got a big fellow, old and tough, but there's plenty."

Marcy and I had pulled young thistles early that morning and it wasn't yet noon. Since the only other thing we had was water, Mama made rabbit stew. The rabbit was clean and healthy. She was worried that she could not make biscuits or corn bread to complete the meal. Jim would expect hot bread, and so would Papa if we had had flour. She lifted the lid to season the stew and the top fell off the can. Black pepper covered the meat. The men looked up. Mama was trembling, biting her lip to hold back the tears. She poured water into a pan, upturned the stew into the water, and washed off the pepper. She replaced the meat in the skillet and started again.

At table, as we ate, our throats burned and we coughed and made jokes. Thistles and the good cold well water soothed us.

Mama said, "Jim, I'm sorry not to have hot biscuits. We're out of flour. Next time you come over, I'll make twice as many."

Jim looked up and around at us all as if he had just noticed our changed appearance. He said very slowly, "You folks all right?"

Papa kicked my bare feet under the table and I touched Marcy's and Mama's ankles with my toes.

"Sure," Papa said. "Buff's got a rock bruise; stepped on a sharp rock. Wonder it hasn't happened before around here. Limps a little but she'll be all right in a day or two. Then we'll go to Artesia."

It was plain that Jim doubted it, but he began to advise Papa about horses. He stayed until midafternoon, and just as he was leaving, Katy and Buff came trotting down the road from pasture.

"You can see she's all over that bruise," Papa said. "They're a fine span of mares."

"You folks come over when Carrie gets back in a couple of weeks," Jim said.

"Thought she wasn't coming back," Papa laughed.

That night after we had gone to sleep, I was awakened by low voices in the other room. Marcy and I slept on our bunks in the kitchen. There was no door between the two rooms. Mama and Papa were talking very seriously, and I heard Mama say, "We've *got* to do something! I know what *I'm* going to do."

"I hate for you to do it," Papa said.

32

THE NEXT MORNING Mama and Papa dressed for going to Artesia. Marcy and I were to stay home for the first time, and we were advised not to play in the canyon or the creek.

"This time of year there might be a flash flood. Play in the house or the yard."

Mama said to Papa, "Well, I guess I'll be the villain." She turned to us. "Girls, I've got to ask you a favor. We need the two quarters Grandfather gave you from Fred's shoulders. Maybe I can get Mr. Starbuck to save them for you and pay him back. We don't have credit there."

We were stunned by this desecration of Fred's memory. We hesitated, even considered refusing, but we understood there was nothing else to do.

We brought our coin purses from the boxes Grandfather had made us, opened the purses, and stared long into them at the lone coins. We took them from their cloth wrapping and handed them over without looking up. They were discolored. We could have given new coins graciously, but to us these were not money, but parts of Fred; they had been lodged in his flesh for many years.

"Good-bye," Marcy said under her breath.

I ran out of the house, forgetting my weakness, and entered the rock room at the yard end of the canyon. The floor of the room was a large flat stone. I lay down and tried to think of our trouble. I was hungry, but all I could think of was that Fred's blackened coins were on their way to be spent for food, the coins Grandfather had given us to keep forever.

Papa was standing at the entrance by the tree that was in bud and that would have red berries in summer.

"Get up from there and go in the house. You can remember Fred without those coins. They're nothing but money." He walked away, and I took my time about leaving. I waited until I heard the wagon drive up onto the plain. When I went in the house, Marcy was in her bunk with her head covered. Being indoors made me more aware of my hunger and of my confused feelings.

Outside, I sat on the ground and looked out over the creek. The earth was waking up. A faint lacy green was in the cottonwoods and all along the far shore. One night soon there would be an explosion of buds, and in the morning the trees would be green, and wild flowers would be nodding in the wind. Already the wind had changed to the southeast; an insinuating soft warmth flowed in its coolness. There was something else in the wind that made me restless.

Now was my chance to go into the canyon. The snakes were probably still asleep or sluggish. I knew better than to walk in the thick brush with its dangers; not all snakes slept in winter, and if they were laying eggs or having baby snakes this early, the mothers might be cranky. I climbed slowly up the path by the barn leading to the garden and walked back on the plain to the edge of the canyon. With one short leap I landed on a boulder and with more strength could have leaped from one to another. The boulder was smooth and warm, as large as a room. I sat down and looked all around at the new sights. A dead bee lay near me. It had come out too early and died of cold. A lizard sunned itself on another boulder. Then I heard a swift delicate sound of running; a horned lizard, which we called a "horny toad," stopped, surprised at such a large intruder. I kept very still. A red ant came up over the side and the lizard's quick tongue darted out; the ant was gone. The lizard was not afraid of me; he neither puffed up nor flattened himself. If I frightened him very much, he might squirt a tiny stream of blood from the corners of his eyes. I had seen that once and it was scary. I longed for a dog, and Papa said if we stayed, Cooper would give us a puppy. In the meantime, I could make a pet of a horned lizard, but I would not take away his freedom. Anyway, I could not bear to provide him with live food. This was another source of long thoughts and confusion: so many of us eating one another. I wanted a horned lizard who would live near the house and be friends. I picked him up and talked to him. What an odd fellow he was! Rough and ugly, with a short heavy tail unlike that of other lizards, he had spines on his head, a blunt nose, and a big lipless mouth that gave him an expression of severity. I did not know the word "prehistoric" but it was possible to sense that he had his beginnings in a time before our own. He blinked and I saw that, unlike a snake, he had eyelids. Eyelids made me think of the great horned owl, its heavy lids, with luxuriant lashes, slowly opening and closing over its motionless eyes. I put the horned lizard down on the warm rock. I wanted an animal pet I could touch with pleasure, one that would respond to my love.

Stretched out in the sun, watching and listening to the life of the canyon, I forgot the hours, until I heard the sound of the wagon from the plain. There was time enough for me to go back the way I came, but I saw that I must leap *up* from my boulder to the ground! I tried my strength by running about on the rock, also to gather momentum, but when I tried to jump, I was afraid of falling into the dark heavy growth below. I remembered what Papa had said: "alive with rattlesnakes." The big smooth boulders were open and safe; there was no place for a snake to hide near me. But I should not have come here at all. And worse, if I managed to get out, I should have to tell a lie, or, I certainly should tell a lie if Papa asked, because he would be very angry that he couldn't trust me. I felt guilty already about the lie I had not yet told. A cunning idea came to me: I should tell Mama or Grandfather and ease my conscience. Suddenly, the sound of the wagon was so near I could hear the horses break into a trot because they were coming home. Without thinking of my inability to leap up, or of snakes below, I found myself back on the

plain running toward the barn, down the steep path. My fearful
energy gave out; the house was still far away. I carried a little
fodder into the barn and dropped it into the manger and went
back for more. This expedient good deed only added to my guilt.
I decided to tell the truth, if asked; if not, my little adventure
would remain a secret. I felt better; and was going along the path
toward the house as the wagon braked down the precipitous road.

Papa didn't ask me anything. He unloaded a can of lard, a
sack each of flour, cornmeal, and pinto beans. Mama held a few
small items of food.

"We'll be all right now," Papa said to me. "We'll have a square
meal. I feel like planting already. Tomorrow I'm going over to
Cooper Loveland's and get my seed."

No one said a word about Fred's quarters.

Papa unhitched the mares and took them to the water tank.
Mama was very quiet; she seemed different. She kept pretending
to be busy getting her things from the wagon when she had them
all in her arms.

"I'll carry something, Mama." When I reached to take a bag
from her hands, I saw it.

A wide white band circled her finger where her wedding ring
had been. I stared. Her blue eyes glistened with tears. She did
not permit the tears to roll down her cheeks but shook her head
once so that the drops flew away.

"Let's go in now and fix something to eat."

33

ONE SPRING DAY when the sweet-voiced mockingbirds were giving repeated notice of their homesites, and doves were cooing madly and bowing before their prospective mates who walked about as if indifferent to the romantic displays, the Claytons arrived with two cross Plymouth Rock hens already setting on their fertile eggs in low boxes lined with straw. The hens were flustered at being moved, but when we placed them in the quiet dugout, cleaned only the day before, they settled down, to appear after that only for corn and water.

"Bought some pullets and a young rooster," Mr. Clayton said, "and that young rooster started fighting old Brigham. Brigham don't take to being penned up, anyway, and he misses the horses."

The elderly rooster was let loose into the yard and stood about as if lost in this once familiar place until he either discovered or remembered the path to the barn. There he stayed, pecking grain from the manger or sorting it out of horse dung. He roosted in the barn and crowed at dawn and sunrise from the roof. Although ours were not the horses of his younger days, he gave them his talkative friendship and was in turn adopted by them. When the eggs hatched, Papa made two small slant-roof houses for the hens and chickens, who were too young to walk up and down the side ramp in the dugout. They explored the yard, two separate families, the fluffy yellow chicks watched over, warned, taught, scolded, and clucked at in affectionate tones. They enlivened the farm. Brigham occasionally looked at them from afar, but remained with the mares. The hens were of little interest to him until they were free of their absorption in motherhood and began laying eggs again, when he would feel called upon to fertilize them.

Papa planted his row crops on the plain and watched over the green shoots as tenderly as the hens over their chicks. He plowed a garden above the rock wall. We dropped seeds, the gift from Carrie, into the moist, rich loam, knowing they would grow and bear. Marcy and I lay down, smelling the new-turned earth, watching the worms wriggle out of the light back into their fragrant dark.

Purple blooms unfolded on the green alfalfa, perfuming the air. The red-berry tree at the opening of the rock room, where we often played, was filled with singing sparrows. Paired mockingbirds played courting games on the clothesline. Meadowlarks fluted their notes from the grass, and buntings trilled everywhere. Hawks sailed above, their long eyesight on the baby chicks and cottontails. The spring days were riotous with the birds' courting songs, the evenings engraved by the mournful mating calls of wolves and coyotes.

Then sounds became early-summer sounds. Birds, now mated, worked to build their nests. We climbed the steep path by the barn, carrying buckets of water to irrigate our garden. Squashes, cucumbers, cantaloupes, and watermelons were sending their runners in all directions. String beans and tomato vines were curling a little in the hot winds. Tired of our plain fare, we could hardly wait for our green vines to mature. We hoed the drying ground and carried more water, a difficult chore; but we were soon rewarded. Birds kept the garden almost clear of insects. If the insects ate some, well, they had to live too. Every morning we climbed to the garden, as much for our pleasure in parting the leaves to see the night's growth of melons as in picking beans and tomatoes we had raised with our own labor.

The horses had learned the way along the ledge and now went to pasture without being led. In the evening Marcy and I followed them up the steep road to watch them roll on the grass, kicking and snorting, before they lunged to their feet and drifted off to crop buffalo grass. We had walked over that pasture many days looking for poisonous locoweed, digging it up and carrying it home in a gunnysack to dry and burn. We were fortunate that our horses were not poisoned or bitten by rattlesnakes. These were not frequent disasters, but they did occur in a land that had always been wild. True, Indians from prehistoric times had roamed and lived upon these plains, and left their culture's artifacts; and just before the white man came with his guns, Cheyenne and Arapaho had warred with Comanche and Kiowa, and all had hunted buffalo. Yet the land was wild and virgin; few had probed its surface, as we were attempting to do.

"Maybe we aren't supposed to open this grass," Papa said. "Maybe the land's fighting back, pushing us off."

We had plowed the grass under, opened the rich unmolested soil, and our dryland crops were growing in the summer sun and hot winds. As we knew from experience, we would have a crop only when it was harvested and sold, not sooner. We knocked on wood when we claimed it earlier and dared not rejoice prematurely.

While we watched and waited and worked, the long hot afternoons of summer began. The pigs withdrew to their cool stone house; chickens panted under the tree. We were quiet with the great weight of the sun, as animals and birds were quiet, resting after courtship and nesting, bearing and rearing. The days themselves seemed lazy and slow, asleep and dreaming.

Day after day Marcy and I crossed the bare yard, our toughened feet burned by the heated stones, to the bank of the creek. We let ourselves down by grabbing exposed roots and by leaping and sliding and falling upon the wet sand or into the stream. There we lay in the shallow water, watching minnows or pretending to swim, naked except for our covered heads, Marcy in her worn straw hat, I in a sunbonnet.

Then, regardless of sun and hot winds, we must all work in the fields. Grandfather's crops ripened a week ahead of ours so we went there to help him, making the long drive at sunrise and sunset. Food from our garden, a watermelon in the water barrel added to our pleasure in going. I begged Papa to let me take a melon to Old Loony.

"You may do it, but he doesn't want us to bother him."

The old man's hut was far from the road to insure no visitors, but Papa drove out of the way. I carried the green watermelon in my arms and placed it beside his door. I knocked. He was there but he gave no sign. Turning away, hearing Papa say, "I told you so," I went back. In a voice that only Old Loony could hear, I said, "Sir Loony! Sir Loony!" He opened the door. Humor showed in his eyes. The pet lizard ran from his shirt pocket onto his shoulder and remained there like a small statue.

"So you remembered Sir Loony?"

I nodded and touched the melon with my bare toe.

"That will taste powerful good," he said. "I thank you. Now wait. I'll get you a present."

He came back shortly and handed me a cloth salt sack filled with something that felt soft and alive. I wished against it, but when I looked in, the coils of dark hair lay like a presence.

"I won't live forever," Old Loony said. He was tough and sturdy.

"Please keep it," I said. "It's yours."

"It's a present. A keepsake."

"Thank you, sir. I won't ever lose it."

"Good day, then," he said and closed the door.

In the wagon, I showed them my gift. Papa said, "He probably killed her, all right."

"No, he didn't," I said.

Mama said, "I can't bear to look."

I planned to keep it in the box Grandfather made for me.

"Will you have to brush it?" Marcy asked.

34

WHEN MAMA CALLED US AWAKE, the windows were still black with night and the oil lamp burned in the kitchen where we slept. The flame had crept up and the glass chimney was smoky. I had forgotten to trim the wick. All but the most necessary household chores could be postponed now; our crops were ripe. Already Papa had left for Grandfather's, where the harvest was not yet completed.

"Breakfast!" Mama sang. "Up! Up!"

We washed, pulled our dresses over our heads, and sat down to thick pieces of corn bread and the dainty pullet eggs we liked.

We were walking across the pasture in the sweet morning air when the sun came up, spreading a waist-deep field of rose fading to pink over the gray land. Our tall shadows moved before us swinging big cane knives and a water jug.

"Watch out for the devil's-claw," Mama said.

Its two claws grabbed a foot, or anything in motion, to scatter its seeds. The sharp points held on. When the plant was dry and woody, its seedpod looked like the delicate head of a bird with a fringe under its throat, but the long graceful claws were like horns.

Three rattlesnakes without heads hung over the fence. So many snakes were in the field that Mama was constantly alerting us. The hiss of the whitish bull snakes only startled us; they were harmless. But the warning rattle, the swift coil to strike, the darting tongue sent us running. Mama bravely tried to unwind the snake with a forked branch she carried tied to her belt. If the rattler refused to leave the row we were working and continued to coil, its powerful movements nearly jerking the stick from her grasp, she cut off its head, and stood trembling. It was terrible to see a live thing so quickly dead.

"But," Mama said, "it's him or one of us." We buried the heads, and later Papa cut off the rattles that told the snake's age and kept them in a box. Snakes were a fine subject of conversation.

Because it was the most valuable, we had pulled the broomcorn first, and Papa had hauled it to Grandfather's farm to be threshed and baled. The broomcorn crop was small but it would pay our debt at Tullery's store in part if not all. We still had to head maize and chop cane.

Before midmorning the sun burned in a white sky. We swung our big knives with skilled ease and laid the cane in piles, to shock it later. Marcy and I liked to play in the teepee shocks, but Mama said it made her nervous knowing the snakes liked to get out of the hot sun under the stalks and leaves. At the end of our rows, we drank from the jug, its wet gunnysack wrapping long ago dried, the water warm. By eleven o'clock we were dusty and tired and hungry. We walked home for our dinner and a chance to lie down before the afternoon's work. No matter how hot the days, summer was nearly over, autumn was not far away, and frost was already a threat.

"By rights, we should be harvesting our garden," Mama said on the way back. "But so far, so good."

White clouds appeared and moved above us on a high wind current. Marcy and I raced their gliding shadows far out on the plain.

Mama called us back. "Better save your strength for work, girls. You can chase cloud shadows when we've gathered the crops."

In the field we spoke little. Once, passing the water jug to Mama, Marcy said, "It's going to be a scorcher."

"Going to be? I am roasted already."

Perspiration ran down our bodies and our faces, making a net-work of rivers on the map of our dust-brown skin. We rubbed our smarting palms with dirt and picked up our knives. Each row completed gave us new pleasure. We looked over the large area of stubble with a sense of wonder at our accomplishment. The uncut crop was a geometric oasis in the immense plain of grass circling us to the horizon. The creek and its trees were not visible from the field.

We quit work just before sundown.

"For some unknown reason," Mama said, "being out on these plains at night makes my skin crawl. It's a ghostly place, although I don't believe in ghosts."

"Should we be afraid?" Marcy asked.

Mama laughed. "No, no. But there's something, a feeling. We'll start walking while there's light."

My promise to Grandfather was once more in grave danger, but I contained my desire to tell about Daft.

"We can't see the stars and the moon unless it's dark," I said, in praise of night.

"True, but I'll look at them from the doorway."

Great white clouds sat around the sky; they were familiar rain-less ornaments. A clump of sunflowers shone in the fence corner. We passed a Scotch thistle with purple tassels. These were the only flowers still in bloom.

"When the stars come out, I will make a wish to stay up night and day," I said.

"I wonder where the wind was today?" Mama asked no one.

It came back the next day and the next, hot, dry, steadily blow-ing. Our lips cracked. Grasshoppers and other insects blew against our faces. Electricity within us seemed to spring out to meet elec-tricity in the air; we had a sensation of crackling. When we brushed our hair in the evening, sparks flew. As we worked in the cane, its leaves curled and sometimes cut our arms. The dry, blow-ing rattle of leaves and stalks obscured the frequent rattle we must fear and heed.

We finished the cane. Papa came home, and we all went into the field to head maize. The burning wind quieted and we had only the heat of the late summer sun. The dry crooked stems broke easily in our hands, the full-grained heads we threw into the wagon, driven by Marcy, brought forth Papa's triumphant praise. Last year's defeat was forgotten.

The next day Grandfather drove into our gate and straight to the field. Bounce trotted under the back end of the wagon in its shade. His long pink tongue, dripping sweat, hung from the side of his mouth. His tail wagged a slow, tired greeting.

"Give that dog a drink!" Papa commanded.

Grandfather climbed down from the wagon, reached for a tin pan he carried, and poured Bounce a drink.

"Goddang my wildcats," Grandfather said, half under his breath. He looked away from the field out over the plain for a long moment. When he turned back, he said, "Ginny, take the team, and you girls drive home. I'll help Walter."

"We won't refuse," Mama said. "Thank you."

Grandfather told Bounce to go with us. Marcy and I boosted the dog onto the wagon and swung onto the back, our legs dangling.

"He is not fond of riding," Grandfather said.

Soon Bounce leaped off, but when we reached home and unhitched Bugs and Dip, the dog went to sleep under the wagon, waking now and then to be sure his friend's possessions were safe.

When the men drove home, Grandfather came into the house first and spoke to us. "I have come to pay you a visit. The reason will be clear, in time."

"Why do you need a reason?" Mama asked.

"Well, I thank ye." He said no more.

When Papa came in from the barn, he said, "On Sunday, we're all going for a ramble."

"Are we going to visit Fred's bones?" Marcy asked.

"Not this time, Sprout."

Long rambles were rare, but on one we walked ten miles to the draw where Fred's bones lay properly rearranged by Grandfather after the wolves and coyotes had dragged them apart.

"It's the limit," Mama said, "when you get so lonesome you have to visit the bones of a poor dead horse. I suppose we'd be visiting the bones of people if they were scattered about."

"In a way, they should be," Grandfather said. "When we cast off our bodies, they should be laid in the earth, clean. That would show the highest respect for them and for the earth."

"Dust to dust," Papa said.

"When the time comes, son, I want that for myself."

"So do I," I said.

"It's probably against the law."

"Oh, mercy!" Mama said. "Do you suppose any of you will be alive to eat this supper I'm trying to fix?"

"I expect to live many a year," Grandfather said. "My people lived long. I have never been sick a day in my life and neither has Walter."

"In the twinkling of an eye, maybe you or I," Papa singsonged.

"Alonzo, we are going up to the garden tomorrow. Would you like to come with us and see our squashes and melons?"

"I would, indeed."

"Dad, you ought to see the angleworms; this soil is rich. Would you believe that a worm has a brain?"

"So I've read."

"Not much of one, but its head has something in it. One of the lowest things on earth, and, by God, it has a brain. I wish I had a few books to read. Sometimes I think I was meant to know a lot more than I do."

"That wouldn't surprise me," Grandfather said.

35

"YOU READY?" Papa came in the kitchen door and stood looking at an old grape basket belonging to Carrie, packed with picnic food, covered with a clean dishcloth.

"Yes, but I will not ride a horse," Mama said. "I am walking over to Carrie's tomorrow for an all-day visit; I don't want to be sore and stiff. Remind me not to forget her basket."

Papa went out and motioned for Marcy and me to follow.

"Why in heaven's name do we have to take the horses on our ramble?" Mama called.

"They'll enjoy it. I saw a picture once of horses running on a beach by an ocean; they were all alone and having fun."

"They'll break their legs getting down into the creek."

"Ginny, I told you we're going way around. You have time to write a letter to your mother and tell her the news. We'll meet you below in about half an hour."

Grandfather was standing in the yard holding the four horses by halter ropes. He swung himself onto Dip's bare back.

Marcy stopped, her face set and stubborn.

"Now what?" Papa asked.

"I won't go if I can't ride with you."

"We'll walk up the road, then we'll ride Buff. She likes me."

Up on the plain I wondered whether to ride Katy or Bugs.

"Katy," Papa said. "Bugs might pitch you off."

Marcy sat behind Papa with her arms around his waist. We rode east above the precipice a long way, down a long slope into the creek, then back on the sand. Mama was waiting. She had let herself down the steep bank the way Marcy and I had all summer. She wore a freshly ironed cotton dress and a sunbonnet as blue as her eyes. Her long sleeves were buttoned at the cuff. In all our country years she had avoided the sun on her fair skin, and now having recovered from sun and windburn in the fields, she was very pretty. The men looked at her with pleasure, and she smiled, accepting.

We dismounted and freed the horses. Papa carried the basket and Grandfather slung the halter ropes over his shoulders. We started back up the creek. The horses stood quietly and drank in the stream.

"Come on!" Papa commanded them. They continued to stand.

Grandfather smacked Dip on his rump, and when the big horse trotted away, Bugs followed, then the mares.

"Damn fools don't know how to enjoy themselves," Papa said.

Mama giggled.

We stopped to look at the swallows' mud nests plastered on the high rock cliff. The birds flew over to look at us, a few so near we saw their pale forehead bands. The wild onions of spring were withered, but tall brown cattails grew in the water. Grandfather told us how he had used them as torches when he was a boy.

Bounce, who had been hunting, suddenly came tearing down the bank and along the sand to join us. Grandfather patted him and said, "Watch the horses!" Bounce kept them moving slowly ahead of us and left them only when Grandfather said, "That's enough. Good boy."

We arrived at a place ideal for our lunch: clean smooth sand under cottonwood shade, with a view of the stream east and west, sparkling in the sun. Doves kept up their quiet summer cooing, and a pair of mockingbirds, middle-aged, heavier than most, long mated, flew about, lighted on rocks, drank from the creek, re-

turned, indicating generally that we were in their territory. As
the sun grew hot, the low whir of insects came from the brush
and the plain.

While we were sitting around the cloth on the sand, eating our
picnic lunch, Papa said, "When we get home, we'll pick a watermelon and eat it for supper." Then, "Well, do you girls want to
hear the news?"

"Mama is going to have a baby, a big-league baseball player,"
Marcy guessed, as if the world were ending.

"We'll see about that sometime," Papa said. "It's nothing like
that."

"It's the cause of my visit," Grandfather said.

"Girls, we're going to town this winter to put you in school."

We were silent, stunned by this news. We liked this place.
Town and people were a fearful prospect; our years in the country had made us painfully shy of strangers.

"I'm so happy I could cry," Mama said. "But we'll miss you,
Alonzo."

"I'll be all right. I'm in my element here."

Papa and Mama exchanged glances at our lack of response.
"We'll get back to our ramble as soon as our meal settles," he
said. "See all we can today."

Released, we jumped up and ran across the creek, exploring
along the rock wall. At the thought of change, every sight and
sound became precious. Out of the wind, the heat was intense.
We threw our clothes on the sand and lay in the water at our old
games of make-believe swimming and building sand obstacles for
minnows to go around.

Papa started the horses and followed them. Farther up the
creek, he called in a loud, lingering voice, "Marcy . . . Marcy."
The words came back to us in an echo, clear, exact, but hollow,
inhuman, as if from some deep and ancient place. We dried in
the sun and dressed quickly to run ahead, to shout for echoes.
Mama and Grandfather added their voices. Bounce barked at us
and at the echoes, and the sound of his barking came back to
confuse him even more. The horses lifted their heads, moved their
ears forward, then back, and having given our antics a moment of
their attention, they returned to grazing along the low south bank.
Such echoes called for better things to say; each of us thought of

words that were beautiful to us; the air vibrated with "murmur,"
"dove," "evensong," "luminous," "sailing," "circle," "feterita,"
"yearning," "flow," and more.

"Song," Mama called, and as we wandered along, she sang.

We applauded and our applause bounced from the rocks.

At a glance there was only the scene of a shining creek with
wide sandy shores, a high rock wall, and a far eroded bank followed by cottonwood trees, their glossy leaves, soon to fall, turning in the wind. But rambling as we were, wandering at ease, we
saw more than we could embrace in one afternoon.

The light was going, the sun gentle and mellow.

"I'd better take the horses up on the plain and they can graze
or go home," Papa said. "Come on, Bounce, round them up, easy,
easy." Papa put a halter on Dip and led him ahead and up the
slope and let him loose. Bounce shepherded the others carefully
over the creek, away from the tumbled rocks, and up the slope.
When he and Papa came back, we praised Bounce, and he
"smiled" his delight, but he waited for Grandfather's nod of approval before he went on his way.

We started back at sundown. The melodious sound of insects
rose as if from one throat, one pair of wings, one set of serrated
legs; it came from the trees, the brush, the plain, undulating in
powerful rhythms.

"Let's get home before dark," Mama said.

"You worried about Indian ghosts?" Papa asked. "Look over
by the creek wall: the lightning bugs."

Their clusters glowed against the shadowed cliff. We walked,
still in the early twilight when the sun's reflected fire made every
leaf and blade, last flower and feather stand out in separate, il-
lumined beauty.

At dusk, the bats flew low overhead. Kildeers ran fast along the
water's edge, taking their evening meal, making their plaintive
cries. Mockingbirds darted for insects. Swallows zoomed up, down,
across, as swift as arrows. Far up the stream, a wildcat drank.

We stopped and looked back along the creek enclosed in dusk,
as if we looked back at our joyful day. Then we climbed up the
darkening bank, holding to rocks and grasping roots.

"It won't be long now," Papa said. "This week the Claytons are
coming out for the chickens. They'll take care of them for us till

spring." He took in a long deep breath of the pure evening air. "I'm going up to get a watermelon while I can still see the garden."

After supper, Grandfather told us a story of old times, of people long dead who lived in our minds as alive as we.

36

"WELL NOW, we've been living four years at over four-thousand-foot altitude and we're going down to around thirty-six-hundred," Papa said in his teaching voice.

The dirt road ahead of our horses and wagon led straight to infinity. The plain was flat and treeless.

"How will we go down?" Marcy asked, fearful of the drop.

"Gradually."

"Our ears will pop," I misinformed her. I was sitting in the back of the wagon on top of a large crate. In the silence of the plain, I could hear the words of Mama, Papa, and Marcy from the high spring seat, the leather sounds of harness, and the steady, pulling rhythm of the horses. Beneath these sounds were the ignoble, protesting grunts of Hannah, the sow, and the cheerful oinks of her son, Prince Pig. Hannah complained about every sway and jolt of the wagon. This confining hay-strewn box was a long way from her clean earthen pen and her very own stone house. However pure and fragrant the air, pig odors assailed me.

But there was no escape. The rest of the wagon was piled high with our few possessions and supplies.

"We will be crossing from Colorado into Kansas," Papa said. "This new town of Elkhart is right in the southwest corner, only a few miles from both the Colorado and the Oklahoma state lines. It's a brand-new town. I kinda like that. Don't you, Ginny?"

"I'm dying to see some people and I hope there's a tree or two."

"Not yet. I heard they set out some little ones, locusts. You'll like a new town, won't you, Marcy?"

"Are you going to stay with us?"

"Sure. Your mother and I want you girls to go to school, get educated, be somebody."

"Ha," I said.

Papa looked back at me. "I'll not have any of that smart-aleck talk. You can speak your mind just as clear with respect as without it."

"I can't stand the idea of wearing shoes again. My feet want to go barefoot."

"Well, you'll wear shoes as soon as we can afford them before school."

"I won't like town. I don't like people," Marcy said, wanting Papa to turn back to her.

"I like animals a lot better," I said.

"Well, my stars!" Mama said. "See what living in this desolate place, never seeing anybody, has done to them!"

"They'll get over it," Papa said.

"I wonder if I ever will?" Mama said.

I loved this wild lonesome country but I liked moving too. And I was sure we'd come back in the spring before school was out to plant new crops. Grandfather was still in his dugout, alone on his dry farm with Bounce and Dip and Bugs.

Toward evening we saw a farmhouse ahead, and Papa said we would ask the farmer and his wife if we might camp in their yard and get fresh water. A windmill was turning and creaking in the wind.

The place had been abandoned. We planned to knock on the back door but it stood open, and the screen door flapped back and forth, its dry hinges rasping. The sun was a clearly round burning star on the western rim of the plains. Long shadows fell dark on the bare yard. Around the windmill and water tank old footprints of cattle and horses, perhaps those of five or six animals, were set deep in the dried mud. A raveling cloth waved frantically from the clothesline. These signs of habitation emphasized the forlorn sadness of the place. We hesitated to enter, then Mama led the way. Odds and ends of furnishings remained and across the top of the old iron stove was written in chalk: STARVED OUT. As we stood, aware of the hard meaning of this familiar phrase, there was a sound from the next room: a thud. We turned, startled. For an instant, a cat stopped rigid in the passage, its hair risen, tail bushed, its wild eyes a silent snarl. It streaked past us in terror and out the back door.

We explored the other room. Thick dust was everywhere, but the wind through the house had kept it fresh, and the cat doubtless disposed of the mice. An old chair remained, its worn cushion colored with tiger-cat hairs. We intended camping along the way, sleeping outdoors, but Mama examined the room and suggested we sleep on the floor.

"The nights now are chilly. We can clean out the dust." Marcy ran to the wagon and brought back her little broom and raised a great cloud sweeping.

Papa said, "I'll unhitch the horses. They're thirsty and hungry and pretty tired. We're lucky to find water. Not much left of ours."

While Mama and Marcy were preparing the room, I went to look for the cat. I found him in the small barn, but he spat at me and would not leave his perch above a manger. I went back to the wagon chuck box for food and utensils to carry into the house. If the cat stayed here, wouldn't he starve?

"I doubt it," Mama said. She was very fond of cats. "I don't think they left him. He wouldn't move or he came back. Cats don't need people but they do like a home."

Nevertheless I was worried about the cat in this deserted place. "He is going back to the wild," I said.

"Well, like us, he wouldn't have far to go. Sometimes I envy that independence."

Papa was coming in the door, smiling. "Now, you know damn well you don't, Ginny."

"Your dad always tells me what I think," Mama said dryly, amiably.

He gave her a quick kiss. I had heard these affectionate, half-
humorous exchanges many times, but some new awareness in me
heard what was submerged, unsaid, not just between Mama and
Papa, but between Jim and Carrie, Mr. and Mrs. Shibley, and, I
guessed, other men and women as well. This knowledge so engaged me that I wandered out again into the yard and beyond
the fence, where I could look over the unbroken distance to the
sun going down. The stillness of the land with its life, secret and
hidden, filled me with melancholy. But there was something
more, and this place and this evening were a part of it. An eye—
not the eyes with which I looked toward the horizon—an eye
within opened for an instant and flashed me a message, a coded
message. How should I ever decipher it? I was a long dimly
lighted passage of doors, doors that were open, ajar, closed. Light
showed under the closed doors. I felt on the verge of a discovery.

The dry buffalo grass crunched behind me, and Papa's foot-
steps came on and stopped about ten feet to the side as if he too
wanted to keep separate. His voice, not speaking to me, went
softly out on the wind.

> When the western sun is sinking
> And your mind from care is free,
> When the whippoorwill is calling,
> Will you sometimes think of me?

He stood there awhile watching the sky change colors and fade
into gray. Somehow I knew he wasn't thinking of any *one;* he
liked that verse, words he had learned and felt long before I
existed in relation to him, words that meant more than nostalgia,
more than they said. He turned abruptly and walked back to the
house. I followed at a distance. A light came on in the windows,
pale at first, gathering radiance in the quick autumn dark. Mama
had lighted our lantern and the deserted house was alive again
for this night.

37

WE DROVE OUT of the yard at dawn. Papa threw the barbed wire gate wide open on the chance that stray cattle or horses needed water. We had seen no animals the day before.

"But you never can tell," Papa said.

Our wagon carried fresh water and the cat. Papa had built a small box from old boards at the barn and bedded it with straw, and Mama had enticed the cat with food and her way with its kind. Out of sight of the pigs, it endured the trip and our company with aloof disregard of us all, later to live a long good life as our pet, especially Mama's, electing to move with us from town to town.

About eleven o'clock we came to a well-fenced farm with dried stubble in the fields and a small herd of cattle grazing on the free range. The house and barn were almost new frame, painted white.

"They don't know what they're in for," Mama said.

"They might make it," Papa said. "You can see they came out here with some cash and they spent it right."

Mama saw the tiny new trees wired down against the wind, and she said in disbelief, "They plan to live here all their lives!"

We stopped our horses outside the gate and Papa went in to ask the woman of the house if she would consider fixing us a hot dinner. "We want to pay you, of course," he planned to say. He came back to the wagon smiling. " 'One dollar,' she said before I could offer. Kind of unusual out here, didn't even give me a chance to show her we weren't asking or begging. Drive in, Ginny. I'll open and close the gate. She's the starched-up kind but she didn't fool me; she's lonesome."

When we knocked on the back screen door, the woman, cool and imperious, handed us some embroidered linen towels and said, "I expect you'll want to wash up." The familiar outside wash bench was along the back wall. We were very dusty and glad for her consideration, but the towels were so fine it was a shame to use them.

"Hope chest," Mama whispered.

When we went inside, the woman showed us into a cold dusky parlor, and since she closed the door, Mama, after hesitating, lay down to rest on a stiff black sofa. Papa was caring for the horses. Marcy and I looked at framed pictures on the walls and old photographs on a round stand covered with a crocheted doily and a huge Bible. On a corner shelf all alone was a photograph of a baby in a casket. The picture's black frame had a black bow on one corner. We looked at this for a long time. "Dead" was awesome, perhaps because we were so young and alive. I remembered Fred, our human friend, and Fred, my horse friend, and all the dead animals and birds and bugs we had seen. I remembered Daft, and wondered if the baby's "pure self" came to visit and if the mother could see it? That gave me goose bumps.

Mama must have been watching us. She said, "I don't know why anybody wants to have anything like that around. Good grief!" She sat up, unpinning her hair, shook and smoothed and recoiled it. Two tears rolled down her cheeks and she brushed them away.

"Lunch is ready," the woman called. Lunch was not a word we used; we had breakfast, dinner, and supper.

In a room off the kitchen, the woman had laid a pretty table. Obviously she had company dishes and silver; they shone on the damask cloth. The ample country food steamed in her best bowls.

At first we were stunned by this display and we were embarrassed as well to sit down in our poor clothes, clean but wrinkled from travel. Then Mama smiled and gave a long sigh, saying, "It's almost like home when I was a girl."

"What are you now, Ginny girl?" Papa asked. He gave Mama a "Q.T." look. "You see, I told you she was lonesome."

The woman came in, surveyed the table, and asked if there was anything else we wanted.

Papa said, "Why, yes, there is, ma'am. Your company."

She was startled and flustered.

"You should eat some of this good meal with us, and we could visit."

"Well, I—no, you folks go ahead." She started for the kitchen, then abruptly turned back. "All right, I believe I will."

Papa got up and brought another chair to the table. Mama praised the food and the setting. The woman sat down, still unsmiling, and pretentiously put bits of food on her plate. Before she took one bite, she leaped up and ran from the room crying, and Mama ran after her. We heard her in a loud, undone, weeping voice, "Oh, this beastly place! I haven't seen anyone for an age, and my husband has gone to the cedars for firewood."

Mama was the right one to console her, and after a bit the two came back to the table and Papa began to tell her about our life in the dugout. Marcy asked for more fried potatoes and I announced that I liked the plains without people.

"I think I used to be a wild horse," I said.

"No doubt," Mama said.

The woman smiled, then giggled freely. "My! My! You have an infidel here."

Marcy, often admonished for speaking with her mouth full, swallowed hard and said, "I saw myself in the water in a buffalo wallow."

"Your reflection," the woman said. "That's nice."

Papa gave us an appreciative look that we recognized as *That's enough, now.* We didn't mind because we suspected it was enough, and besides, we wanted to eat unnoticed.

Just before we left, Mama asked the woman for milk to fill the cat's bowl.

"Mercy, yes. He may as well have cream."

Papa had placed the silver dollar on the kitchen table on his way out to hitch up the horses. When the woman saw it, she protested but held the coin. Mama understood very well and urged her to keep it.

"It *is* nice to have a little money of one's own," the woman said. "So unexpected, too. I prayed only for a human voice."

"You got four," Mama laughed.

At the wagon, the woman gave us a loaf of bread she had baked that morning. "I'm Mrs. Portis. I was so addled I forgot to say." We had introduced ourselves at first. "Mrs. Rex Portis."

"Why, that's the name of our son," Papa said. "Rex."

I saw Mama nudge him to keep still.

"If you ever come this way again—" Mrs. Portis said.

"If you come to Elkhart this winter, the latchkey's out. We'll stop on our way back at planting time."

We drove away amid these sincere pleasantries.

"We exchanged addresses," Mama said.

"General Delivery, U.S.A.," I sang, knowing I shouldn't, but I could not resist.

Papa did not turn around, but he spoke to Mama as if puzzled. "I wonder what's come over Cheyenne?"

"Eleven years, I guess," Mama said.

The sun was just a little to the west of the blue sky's zenith.

"We'll camp out tonight," Papa said. "And by tomorrow afternoon we ought to be there." He looked back at me sitting on the pig crate. "Do you notice that I cleaned out the pig pen?"

38

THE COOL BLOWY MORNING turned into an Indian summer afternoon. The heat tired us all. Papa slowed the horses. On that great expanse of buffalo grass we were a plodding target for the sun. Mirages appeared ahead on the road: shimmering silver lakes of such beauty that they could only be ephemeral. By early evening, sagebrush grew thicker to the north of us, and Mama, longing for the woods and brooks of her childhood, said she thought the land was rising.

"A little," Papa said. "The Cimarron River runs along through some low hills just there."

"Let's cut across and camp there tonight. Hills and a river!"

"It'll be dry now. And by sundown the horses will be too tired for side trips. We'd better stay on the road."

The road was two shallow wheel tracks with grass in the center. It was used, Papa told us, from his store of histories, by farmers within a hundred miles hauling their broomcorn to the railroad. "They come from all these border states, Colorado, New

Mexico, Texas, Oklahoma. Of course, they don't all use this road."

"Where *are* these farmers?" Mama asked.

"Oh, scattered around. These are big plains. A good many little towns ahead. Eastern speculators tried to boom this country a couple of times, going to build cities, railroads, bought and sold a lot of land, and many a poor devil paid cash and then lost his shirt. This country will be rich someday. I'd like to own a few thousand acres in any of it."

"Oh, mercy," Mama said.

"Elkhart is a boom town because of the railroad. It's the end of the line."

"Is it?"

"Ginny, when we make some money, you go home for a visit, and when you come back, you'll like these plains. You'll see. They get in your blood."

Mama would not commit herself, and although her remarks about plains and farming were sincerely felt, they were spoken in her gentle, half-humorous way, and Papa, in the guise of good-natured acceptance, ignored them.

"I am awfully glad we'll be on a railroad though."

That satisfied Papa.

We pulled off the road and made camp, working in the abruptly cold, brilliant air of sunset. Papa circled our camp with a rope laid on the ground against rattlesnakes.

"This might be just a superstition but we're taking no chances."

A tangy autumn fragrance rose from the dun grass and sagebrush and from the earth itself, richly fertile and dry—a tang of arid places.

While Papa was busy with the horses and pigs, Mama made our beds on the ground and fed the cat. Papa dug a shallow hole and built a fire, a fire we guarded carefully lest it spark a prairie blaze. We had brought wood from the deserted farm as there was nothing but grass and a little brush on the plain. Our supper of fried potatoes and onions, eaten in the open as we sat cross-legged around the fire, tasted better than any indoor meal. A nighthawk wheeled above us in the dusk, and in the immense silence a meadowlark sent up its beautiful song.

"This is the life," Papa said.

I felt as joyful as the meadowlark and as free. Marcy was taking in the beauty, keeping it to herself. Mama's eyes were dreaming; perhaps she was storing this peaceful time, or imagining our new home tomorrow. We sat for a long time without speaking, then Papa said, "We'd better enjoy this old night all we can. It may be the last one like it unless we come back in the spring."

Was Papa already thinking of other places after Elkhart? Was this good-bye to Baca County, to the dugout, to the beautiful, rocky shelf on the creek? To Grandfather? No, not to Grandfather. He and Papa, all their lives, would be joining and parting and joining again. I knew that much.

After washing our pans and banking the campfire, we lay in our heavy comforters, the clumps of buffalo grass poking our backs.

"This is the life," Mama teased Papa.

Just then a mockingbird sang out from the north and Papa said, "There must be a few drops of water in that river after all."

Vega was the first big star to appear in the dusk directly over our heads. The long twilights of summer were gone and in the quick autumn dark we began to look for stars and planets. It was hard to keep up with the roaming planets and constellations, but if we could find a constellation we could depend on its stars to be in place. If Grandfather were here he could help us.

"You can't miss the Big Dipper this time of year," Papa said.

Marcy crawled over me and hit Papa with her small fist. "Don't tell. Let us find them first!"

"All right, then, pard, find the Horse and Rider, test your eyesight."

The Milky Way swarmed across the sky, and in the clear, moonless dark such countless stars shone with brilliance that we had to look for a time before we could find the Big Dipper that Papa thought we couldn't miss. Then, in the handle of the Big Dipper we found a bright star with a tiny dot "riding" on it. That was the Horse and Rider, our triumph and proof of perfect sight. We traced the geometric constellations with our fingers in the dark, but we could not begin to name them.

I fell asleep hearing the hobbled horses cropping grass, and the voice of coyotes not far away. I made a wish never to live for long where I could not hear the mockingbird, the meadowlark, and the coyote.

39

NEW LOTS AND STREETS marked on the virgin plain signaled with small strips of cloth fluttering from stakes. New lumber lay in piles, and from the heart of the town the lively sound of workmen hammering nails came to us on the wind. Upon entering the town proper, we were surprised that it was larger than we had expected. Hundreds of people lived in neat houses surrounding the main street, and a large square brick building rose an extra story above the town: the school.

"Oh! let's drive up Main Street before we settle," Mama urged, and Papa reined the horses.

Mama saw the post office first. She had redirected our mail and could hardly wait the several days until letters arrived. Cars were parked in the center of the street, horses and wagons in vacant lots. We plodded along, looking from left to right so as not to miss seeing all the places of business: hardware, bakery, drugstore, bank, stationer, dry goods, real estate, feed and grain, two cafés, a few other shops that catered to the basic needs, and a large general store from which the music of a player piano near the door deluged the street. Several customers gathered around the piano were singing "There are smiles that make us happy, there are smiles that make us blue, there are smiles . . ." We passed by and saw the newspaper office, and farther on, past a one-story hotel, the railroad station and its tracks marked the end of the town. It was a good town.

Papa bought a paper, the *Tri-State News*, and we headed in the general direction of the school. In sight of it, just beyond a lumber yard and a coal company, we turned into a large open square surrounded with low barns, harness rooms, and bunk-houses. Two covered wagons were at one end, horses in corrals and cow ponies tied to wooden rails. The whole place had the good smell of horses. It was called simply Feed Yard.

"We'll have to stay here a few days until we can rent a house," Papa said. "As soon as we sell Hannah and the shoat, we'll have a little cash. Poor old girl." He went to see about the rent and came back, saying we'd stay, and that the owner was a good fellow and told him he could keep the pigs in one of his pens, and he would help Papa find a buyer, which wouldn't be hard. "I told him I'd only sell her as a brood sow. Prince won't be so lucky, poor devil."

"He wouldn't have been any luckier on the farm," Mama said, just as my resistance to towns was increasing.

"Will we have to sell the horses?" I asked, near tears.

"That depends," Papa said, which seemed to me a mysterious remark. "If I can get work right away and we go back to Colorado in the spring to plant, or if we can find a house on the edge of town, we can keep them."

The edge of town was no more than two or three blocks from Main Street; my hopes rose.

Papa looked at me very seriously. "They'll need oats and hay and plenty of exercise."

"Marcy and I will exercise them, Papa!"

"Well, we'll see what we can do."

A roustabout came over to help, and the two men unloaded the pigs, took the horses to their stalls and rubbed them down. We cleaned out the wagon bed, shifted our belongings, and put down fresh hay, and Mama made our beds. We would all sleep in the wagon.

"School has already started, girls. Tomorrow we'll figure out how to get a bath and get into clean clothes, and go enroll."

"What grade will I say?" I asked.

"I don't know. You've been out of school since the first grade in Oklahoma, remember. Grandpa has taught you a lot, but we'll have to see what they say."

"Well, I won't be with little kids, that's final."

"Be polite. You're already smart, but don't get the bighead, miss."

It pleased me to be praised for my intelligence. If I had been pretty once and would be again, there was nothing attractive now about my extreme thinness, sunburned skin, and the half-starved look of my big-eyed face and dried hair. Marcy was in the same fix but she was younger, and I wasn't sure that she minded when people stared at her.

Mama was looking at our feet.

"Fall weather and barefoot!"

"I'm glad." I didn't know that living in town would change my opinion, but at least in summers I could still go barefoot.

Marcy was very quiet, and I knew she was afraid of the next day and school. She was a sensitive little girl, painfully shy. She was Papa's girl, fearful of separation, alert to default. I was afraid myself, but I was curious and eager for new experiences.

When Papa came back, we ate sardines and crackers and went to bed in the wagon with its high sideboards enclosing us. We could hear horses and see the stars, but the sounds of town were too near.

"Next month you can see Jupiter," Papa said, and it seemed to me I heard it in my sleep and that Grandfather, not Papa, was saying it.

We sat in the superintendent's office waiting.

"Don't look so scared," Mama said. "I'm so glad, I could cry, to get you kids in school."

We heard a loud thump, step, thump, step, thump, in the hall. A tall severe man in a black suit thumped in. His right foot was in a huge black shoe. He removed his black derby hat, hung it on the coat-tree, sat at his desk, and recognized our presence. The red band on his forehead made by his derby emphasized the cold gray of his prominent eyes, and although we learned in time that he was a kind, though strict man, that day his sober, waiting expression almost petrified us. Mama, gentle and courageous, explained briefly.

"No problem about the little one," he said, "but the older one will have to start in the second grade and be passed to where she belongs, or"—he glanced at me and must have noted my stricken reaction—"or perhaps she can be given a series of oral and written examinations instead. Miss Temple will be the one to do this." He rang a little handbell on his desk and a woman appeared from the next room. "Get Miss Temple, please. She's upstairs in Ancient History."

I knew nothing of Ancient History, and my throat closed over the thank-you I intended. Mama gave it.

"That's in high school," he said, "but Miss Temple has taught all grades. Miss, who is the President of the United States?"

"Woodrow Wilson, sir."

"Fine. Are we at peace or war?"

"I am not sure, sir."

He nodded and said nothing more. Miss Temple opened the door and leaned in.

"Do come in and close the door, Miss Temple. I am aware that you are in class."

"Oh, sorry, Professor Waite, sorry, sorry!" She came in, a tiny, merry, homely woman, middle-aged, but her manner making her seem almost as young as my mother. She had red hair braided and coiled; a strand kept falling in her eyes and once she frowned, bit the strand, and said under her breath, "Curse!"

"That will do, Miss Temple."

"*Your* hair is short," she laughed.

"That will do. Now, let's get to the problem." He explained.

"Oh, glad to! If Miss Thomas and Mr. Reedy can take over study hall tomorrow, we could start then."

"I'll attend to that, then. Thank you, Miss Temple." He nodded to me. "Nine in this office."

The lower grades were in a flat new building in the same large bare treeless yard, and there I walked with Marcy the next morning before nine o'clock. She was already a good student and would be ahead of her age group, but being shy, she needed an advantage, as the teacher had pointed out to Mama the day before.

Marcy was clutching her new collapsible drinking cup and first wanted a drink from the school hydrant near the back door. We passed a playground marvel and vowed to try it next day. It was a tall heavy pole with a wagon wheel on top, and suspended from the wheel were long ropes looped at the end. A child grabbed a loop, ran around until airborne; as more and more children did the same, the wheel gathered momentum and they flew higher and higher in the air in a circle. It was a rather dangerous game but that was no matter if one could get into the air. Two home-made teeter-totters and a metal slide stood between the buildings and were shared by all. The slide was almost as miraculous as the wheel. A hard-running game between two straight-line bases was going on with loud calls, yells, and laughter. Without a word to each other, we took all this friendly noise in and agreed that school and town were less fearsome than we had imagined. It was even possible that in a few days we should be a part of these unaccustomed numbers.

Miss Temple was astounded that I could have learned so much from reading only *The Adventures of Kit Carson* and a collection of tales and poems. I tried to explain to her about Grandfather, but she sped on to questions and problems and discovered gaps in my education that made her frown. I expected to hear her say "Curse!" but she looked hard into my eyes and asked, "Will you study like a house afire?" This reminded me of Grandfather's examples. I said yes. She looked at my bare feet and asked, "What about buying school books?" I said that we would get them. "Sure?" I nodded yes. She made a list. "I can get my hands on some old ones for you today to fill in those holes in your learning, and you can catch up. Fast, though."

"We will pay for them, too," I said, trained in pride.

"No you won't! They're just moldering in the office."

"Thank you. I'll study hard."

"Now, listen here, young lady. I'm going to try you in the seventh grade. You're ready. It's harder than the eighth, which you can doubtless skip into high school. Stay home a few days and study every minute. I don't want you to be embarrassed in class."

I would have stayed up night and day for her. I was already planning how I could light the lantern in Katy's stall and study there. I could sit in the manger or find a stool, or even sit astride Katy's broad back.

"Where do you live?" Miss Temple startled me.

"At the Feed Yard."

For an instant she behaved as if everyone lived in a Feed Yard and I was uncomfortable with this pretense. Then she burst out laughing, and when she could speak, she said, "My dear, you are priceless. First, it's *The Adventures of Kit Carson* and now . . . well, no one at home believes any of my letters . . ."

Somehow I knew she wasn't laughing at me but simply enjoying all the new experiences that came her way, and I understood that.

"Are you from Back East?" Back East was a completely foreign place.

"I was. But this is my home, my true home. I knew it the moment I laid eyes on it. I must have been here before."

This stirred my curiosity but I was afraid to pry.

"Soon," she said, "you'll be reading the poets. They have that sense. And Emerson. You can read Emerson all your life and keep finding new things as you grow. He isn't at all the stuffed shirt people think he is."

I put her words away to get them out at another time. There was something familiar here. An image of Daft came to me. Who was Emerson?

40

THE TRAIN CAME IN the late afternoon. After being washed, inspected, and given necessary care, it switched to its return position and left that night at 9:05. There was something impressive about that train pulling out at "05," not a minute before or after. Depending on the season, it hauled broomcorn and cattle to Kansas City and brought in a variety of merchandise, new people, and mail. Of the three, the mail appeared to be the most important. As soon as the mailbags were dragged into the post office, people gathered and talked and waited—mostly waited without talking—for the postmaster and a helper to put up the mail. In this town and others to follow, it was I who went for the mail, one of the best of pleasures.

At first we stood in the sun's late glow, then the dusk, and when we could hardly see one another, the electric lights came on. Low-watt bulbs hung from the ceiling, their filaments showing through clear glass, the dim light adding to our intimate expectations and anxieties. Men spoke of the new electric power plant

made possible by the war boom. Although I brought along a
school book to study, I spent part of the time looking at people
who waited and those who continued to drift in and out. There
was talk outside on the sidewalk, but in the post office there was
now almost complete silence as if everyone was listening to the
significant whisper and slide of letters and papers being sorted
and placed in boxes and cubbyholes. Townsmen unlocked num-
bered boxes, drew forth mail, and waited for more. I wished that
one day we could afford a box. I imagined turning the dial lock,
which would open only when one remembered the secret numbers
and how to turn to them, forward and back.

Every evening I waited for the mail, I waited also for the regu-
lar appearance of three very pretty young women who were so
exactly alike that I could not distinguish one from another. They
were pale and they wore their tawny hair in an extravagant style
new to me. When they entered the post office, it was as if this
appearance were the most important social engagement of their
day and evening. They had many dresses and shoes, all expensive
and beautiful, and from head to toe they were immaculate like
new dolls right out of a box. They walked straight to the same
place every evening, stood against a wall, a space that seemed to
be reserved for them. If a stranger stood there, he moved. I
stared at those six green eyes that looked with arrogance at everyone and no one. The girls spoke only to one another in low voices.
Other women seldom came to the post office at this hour; they
were cooking suppers. But when one did come in, the three young
women watched her every moment and their brilliant eyes were
saying, "I'm just as good as you are."

These young women fascinated and puzzled me, and I must
have stared at them too openly and too long, for one evening a
rough man standing near nudged me with an elbow. When I
turned, he said, "Don't get any ideas, sis. They're sure purty but
purty is as purty does."

"What?"

"Just keep your distance."

"Are they rich?"

"Hell, no," he drawled. "They're whores."

My eyes opened wider; I had already heard from a big girl at
school what that word meant.

"Floozies. Ladies of the Evening. Got it?" the man said. "Can't

you tell that? Their eyes and lips painted. Their faces like they fell
in a flour bin. They got their sign out, see, and they don't need
to say a word. That's a lesson to you. Now you look out. Next
time you'll know. I saw you gettin' too interested."

"I'm not! They're just so pretty."

"Purty, hell!" He spat.

"Well, thank you."

"Don't mention it."

A small wooden clatter sounded. People moved into a loose
line. The general delivery window opened with a second clatter.
A wave of sheathed excitement flowed in the air. Many men received one letter; those who received none turned from the line
with blank faces as if to cover their disappointment. When it was
my turn, I said, "Babb, please." The postmaster smiled at me,
took a packet of letters from the "B" cubbyhole, sorted through
them one by one, and handed me three and a picture postcard.
I saw with delight a thin letter from Grandfather; the others were
for Mama. The Triplets were standing behind me and I enjoyed
their perfume. Living in the Feed Yard, studying nightly in a stall
with Katy, who nibbled at me and crowded me, affectionate, and
impatient with the lantern light, I may have smelled a little of hay
and horses, but that was a good smell too.

After three weeks in the Feed Yard, Papa got a job as a baker,
the trade he knew, and we moved to rooms attached to the bakery.
He decided to keep Katy and Buff in the care of the Feed Yard
until spring crop-planting time. Marcy and I visited them whenever we wished on our way to or from school. By really cold
weather we had shoes and winter coats. Papa had bought Mama
a good secondhand sewing machine from the owner of the bakery,
and Mama had made us each three pretty dresses. We even had
ribbons for our hair.

"There's only one fly in the ointment," Papa told us. "This
bakery being owned by a bossy woman. No wonder her husband
up and left her. Working for a woman damn near unmans me.
But we need the money."

The truth was that Papa liked only to work for himself; he dis-
liked all jobs. "I like my independence. If I can make some extra
money someway, I might buy the old hussy out." Before his
attempt at farming, he had owned small bakeries with his father
or on his own and avoided working for other men.

In spite of his chagrin, he was full of his own life that bloomed in towns among men. He was a man who got up in the mornings *living*, and you could see him living, enjoying, interested in everything small and large, in everyone, all day. This brought him a popularity he had missed on the farm; but he was restless in town in a way he had not been in the country.

The bakery occupied a long narrow third of a building that housed the *Tri-State News*. This lively, intelligent newspaper was edited and published by a woman and her four handsome sons, the Smiths. In this instance, Papa was filled with admiration for Mrs. Smith, for her intelligence and ability, to which he added: "She's a real woman, too, not trying to act like a man." We became friends. And, fortunately for us all, the more commonplace woman owner of the bakery retired to her house and left the shop to be run by Papa and Mama. After school, Marcy and I carried between us a large metal basket in which we delivered bread to White's General Store, the hotel, and the two cafés. We were then released to study, to read, to play the long evening games after supper. Our chief game, "Run, Sheepy, Run," kept us and twenty other children running, hiding, calling all over one end of the little town.

At home there was the fragrance of baking bread, and for me, the magnetic sight of the paper-jumbled news office and the steady sound of the presses that some nights lulled me to sleep on my packing-box bed.

41

OUR LIVES CHANGED so much in just a few months that even though we had come to a new town still in the southwest plains, we were back in the world. Before, we had lived on the earth; now, we lived in the world. And the world was in feverish change.

And the town was changing with it. From the cheerful building of homes, the pride in piped water and electric lights and the paving of Main Street, the work and pleasure of people going about their lives and of families growing up as the new trees grew, the town turned restless; it had caught a fever from afar. Men argued and sometimes fought in the streets against the business of war and saving the world for democracy. Many spoke with anger of the warring German Huns. The player piano at White's General Store appealed to all passersby with the emotion of "Over There." Customers sang with the piano: " . . . oh, the Yanks are coming, and we won't come back till it's over Over There."

Not all agreed. "Let old Europe settle her own quarrels. They'll always be at war." Words were exchanged. Fists were raised. And where men used to fight in the soft dust of Main

Street over personal matters, they now fell hard on the pavement and swore over nations.

One day Mama ran from the bakery to our small living quarters in back, crying, "I hate politics and war!" She had just received a letter from her youngest and favorite brother that he had volunteered to go to France.

I wasn't sure what war meant, but it seemed oddly a gay occasion for bands, urgent songs, the excitement of new adventure. And killing. I could not kill a grasshopper. He had eyes, he looked at me, and his eyes said: "This is my life." I respected that. Had this no place in the grown-up world? Pictures of young boys who had been killed or crippled appeared in the *Tri-State News*. I cut them all out and placed them gently in a small folder that advertised seeds. Marcy and I were going to plant cosmos flowers along the back wall. The folder stated they were hardy enough to grow in arid places.

One evening Papa said that we were to be dressed and ready to go to the train at eight o'clock. "It's a troop train," he said, "or almost. No civilians going out tonight. A lot of boys from here and farms and towns around; from training camps. They're shipping out, the poor devils."

The whole town was there, but we had walked to the station early, and stood on the platform near the train, three coaches jammed with boys in uniform, with officers at the doors to keep order. Papa held Marcy on his shoulders so that she would be safe from feet. Mama stayed close to Papa; she didn't like crowds. Her face was sad with thoughts of her brother. I was free to look out for myself. Mrs. Smith was there, standing close to a window talking with her two oldest sons, on their way to training camp.

All the train windows were open, and boys three and four deep hung over the sills, all but falling, or squeezed among others, calling and waving to relatives and friends and strangers. They appeared to be gay. They looked better in their uniforms than in overalls or suits; and it seemed that these uniforms gave them a sense of confidence and importance. Assembled and trained to kill, they were already separate from all of us on the platform. I could not understand this but I had heard it said. It was true. It was unbelievable. When this thought came, I looked for signs that might reveal this terrible fact. But there were only laughing faces, and here and there one taut with shyness.

The faces of parents were smiling too, but their smiles were untrue. They were trying to be brave. I had been told that was a good thing to do: Don't cry; be brave, be a big girl. But some of the big girls were crying openly.

The first train whistle blew. The band, which had been waiting for this signal, exploded into a rousing patriotic march. The whistle had another immediate effect. Girls and young women rushed from the crowd to the windows, and several of them, crying, pushed the officers at the doors aside and boarded the train. Those alongside reached their arms up and boys reached down, brothers, sweethearts, strangers. The girls flung themselves toward the boys; they smiled and wept and kissed. Some kissed only the ones they loved; others kissed one soldier, then another. A girl who had got on the train threw her arms around a shy stranger from a farm or another town and kissed him. I saw his face redden, then smile. The parents were kept back by the girls, not by intention, but, as Grandfather would have said, by another of nature's designs. The parents did not interfere; they stood back and waved, and smiled with strained faces. They did not frown or scold the girls for their public abandon.

I was only an observer. I watched all the kissing, the eyes shining with love and stunned with grief, and I imagined myself a part of this night's drama. I had not thought much of being a girl in relation to boys, but the daring kisses woke a nebulous longing in my body and mind.

The train whistle blew a second time, and a trainman sang, "All aboard!" The girls who were aboard leaped down and ran alongside with all the others, holding hands, then touching fingers with the boys as the train moved away from the station. The people stayed on the platform. The train gathered speed and sent a long, sorrowing whistle back over the plains. At a cattle crossing it whistled once more; then only the low, steady rhythm of the wheels on the rails came back like a pulse on the high clear air. The people began to leave. The musicians broke their pattern and became ordinary men going home.

Papa put Marcy down. "You're too big to carry." She was half-asleep. He took her hand as if she were a tiny girl and she held on for the three blocks home. "She'll be grown up before we know it," he said.

"I never want a son," Mama said. "Why can't we just live our lives, every last one of us?"

"Well, when you come to think of it," Papa said, "I guess that's what we're all doing."

As we passed through the bakeshop to our quarters, he said, "I've got to punch that dough down." The rising bread dough in the long, clean wooden trough was pushing against the lid, hanging over the side. "It's sure full of life tonight."

While we got ready for bed, Papa scrubbed his hands and arms, tied on a white apron, and tackled the dough. We could hear him striking the resisting mass with his fists, lifting it up a few feet at a time and throwing it over and punching it again. When it was subdued, he replaced the lid. By sunup the dough would have risen again, tilting the lid, as if eager to be out and rolled into loaves and baked in the huge brick oven. That was its life, I thought.

Lying awake on my box bed, I thought of all I had seen that night. I felt vaguely aware of a principle of life: Opposites were everywhere; there would not be one without the other and none was the same. One night was darker than another, one day more brilliant, one sound in a thousand sounds, one silence deeper.

The silence I loved most was that of wild, lone places. It was powerful with the whispered sounds of being. The earth had other wildernesses but I knew only the plains. They made me lonely for something unknown, for something before time began. Perhaps we never would live on those plains again. So little and yet so much had happened since we had left them that I knew going back would not, ever, be the same. Our lives had been changing all along and I hadn't noticed.

Those young farm-boy soldiers on the train were already changing and the ones to come back (and the ones who would not) would be changed even more. And the girls. The parents. The town. And the world.

I was changing, too. It's all right, I thought sleepily. Everything has to grow. Trees and—I fell asleep thinking of the little trees on this treeless plain, growing in the strong winds, winds that howled and winds that sang. I liked the winds. I liked being alive.